SOCIAL ENTERPRISE

HOW TO SUCCESSFULLY SET UP AND GROW A SOCIAL ENTERPRISE

Any advice provided in this book is for general guidance only and you should seek professional legal, accounting and financial advice based on your individual circumstances and the circumstances of your social enterprise about what action to take.

First published October 2016.

Printed in the United Kingdom.

ISBN 978-0-9957486-1-3

When one feels pulled to do a particular thing, when one has passion for a certain life path, karma is always involved. In such an instance, when the goal is worthy and makes one happy, one should continue on that same life path. Just because the elephant cannot carry you anymore doesn't mean you should give up your goal. Continue down the path that makes you feel fulfilled. Those who continue on an unrewarding path for the sake of only monetary gain are displaying a lack of trust in life. *Kwan Yin*

This book is dedicated to my son Lewis, who is full of joy and happiness. I wish you all your dreams and more.

THANK YOU

Thank you to the following people who supported my crowdfunding campaign so this book could be published:

My Mum and Dad, Melissa Chand, Cheryl Garvey, Siobhan Harper-Nunes, Monica Douglas-Clark, Patricia Gomez, Ruth Holt, Victor Shaw, Pauline Roche, Kinga Ko, Bev Reid-McPherson, Rae Sinclair, Birgit Kehrer, Brian Hendrick, Leone Martin, Eleni Paschou, David Preston, Jo-Anne Fisher and Jacqi Eagles.

Thank you to my parents for encouraging me and reminding me not to give up. Thank you to the various people I have met and learnt about social enterprise from over the past 18 years, and to Penny Newman OBE, Jean Jarvis MBE and Melanie Bryan OBE who have inspired me to think bigger and make more impact. Finally, thank you to all the people who have contributed case studies to this book.

About Heidi Fisher

Heidi has a passion for enterprise, having set up and run several charities, social enterprises and businesses over the past 18 years. Heidi is passionate about helping people to change their lives and their businesses, by identifying the growth points in their businesses and unblocking peoples' issues around abundance, money and success.

Heidi's background is as a Chartered Accountant, having initially trained with PwC, and she was the Founder of Harris Accountancy Services CIC – a specialist social enterprise and charity accountancy firm, which she ran for eight years, before selling it in December 2015.

Now Heidi runs Make an Impact CIC which helps organisations to become sustainable through trading, to secure social investment and to effectively report the difference they make with Social Impact and Social Return on Investment reports.

Heidi has worked with hundreds of social enterprises, ranging from start-up enterprises through to those with over £1 billion of income. This includes all different sectors including community organisations, business support, youth projects, sport, drug and alcohol services, ex-offender services, education and employment initiatives, art and culture, as well as health and social care.

Heidi regularly delivers workshops and training on social enterprise, social investment, social impact measurement and finance. Heidi also speaks at events on these subjects and gives back to social enterprises by being on the Boards of a number of organisations. More recently Heidi has set up the Lewis Enterprise Foundation, as a charity, to support 100,000 children around the world to move out of poverty by enabling their families to set up sustainable enterprises. The charity is named after her son, and is part of her commitment to leaving a legacy and a better world for her son to grow up in. 50% of profits from this book are being donated to the charity to support its work.

GET IN TOUCH

You can get in touch with Heidi:

Heidi@HeidiLFisher.com www.HeidiLFisher.com
www.lewisenterprisefoundation.org
www.twitter.com/heidilfisher
www.facebook.com/makeanimpactcic
Join Heidi's Facebook Group for advice and support with your social enterprise:
www.facebook.com/groups/socialenterprisesuccess

CONTENTS

Foreword

By Penny Newman OBE

I first met Heidi five years ago. I was interviewing for a Finance Director. I was the newly appointed CEO running a charity that supported vulnerable and disadvantaged women in the UK. I was seeking to find an experienced and skilled finance person, but one who could make management accounts come alive and be understood by the many managers and others who find numbers to be alien and to be avoided.

The first impression was of a quietly spoken person, who answered the questions with precision and firmness, and one who certainly ticked the box regarding relevant qualifications, including a knowledgeable understanding of social enterprise. However my interest was heightened when she told me about her time as a teacher and her ways of working with her pupils, including those that were not interested in her topics! In addition, Heidi demonstrated two other attributes throughout the interview – an immense passion for social justice and a wicked sense of humour! I had found my ideal candidate.

With her help we produced a successful plan to turn the charity's financial situation around, with individual staff understanding and appreciating financial as well as social outcomes.

Heidi's style of directness and easy fluency permeates this book, and you can pick it up and find illustrative case studies supporting important points throughout. Social Enterprise: How to Successfully set up and grow a Social Enterprise is an enjoyable and informative read. I just wish this book had been around when I started my career in social enterprise.

Penny Newman OBE

INTRODUCTION

This book has been written to assist you with setting up and growing a social enterprise. The book highlights the key areas where social entrepreneurs typically get stuck. It is designed to take you through each of the issues you will face.

SECTION ONE

This section is about understanding what a social enterprise is; linking what your organisation will do with your passions; developing the business plan; taking care of yourself and deciding on your legal structure.

SECTION TWO

This section is focused on creating, developing and pricing your products and services; how to budget and manage your finances and effective ways to market your organisation.

SECTION THREE

This section looks at how you can finance your social enterprise; the social investment options and available tax reliefs; the key issues with VAT; how to measure and report on your social value; exit strategies and the future of social enterprise.

SECTION ONE

CHAPTER 1: WHAT IS SOCIAL ENTERPRISE?

A way of doing business

Let's dispel a myth straightaway – social enterprise is not a legal structure. Social enterprise is a way of doing business that benefits more than the shareholders/owners of the business. Other terms used to describe a social enterprise are mission led or purpose led businesses, but this does not include ordinary businesses that simply do something good in the community through their corporate social responsibility programmes. To count as a social enterprise there must be something written in to the governing document or rules that the business operates by that cannot be changed so it is always a social enterprise.

Social enterprises have a social, economic, community or environmental purpose at their core – for example, providing taxis that run on solar power rather than diesel, which reduces CO_2 emissions and our carbon footprints; a consultancy business that employs ex-offenders; a healthy eating educational programme; art painted by ex-gang members; mobility equipment for people with disabilities. But let's be clear about one thing – anything you buy – products or services – or which may be available in the future – can be provided through a social enterprise. There are no restrictions on what social enterprises can provide.

Making money

The next thing about social enterprise, which is where a lot of people come unstuck, is that it should generate surpluses (or profits). Social enterprise is not about doing things for nothing, it is not about getting funding – delivering a project and then stopping that project because the money has run out or chasing after the next pot of money. Social enterprise is about being sustainable right from the start, or having a clear plan to become sustainable rather than remaining grant dependent.

Many people believe that social enterprises can rely solely on grant funding to deliver their social purpose, but this is effectively being a charity or voluntary organisation, as the delivery model lacks enterprise, as you do not trade anything, you have no products or services – you just deliver projects.

Grant funding makes your organisation incredibly unsustainable as you can never build up reserves, and you are dependent on a funder saying yes for you to continue in existence. But if you make money just think how many more people you can help and how much more social change you can achieve with those surpluses, versus an organisation that makes no money and is continually limited by what grant funding is available.

The only times grant funding is right for a social enterprise is in three circumstances - when the grant programme is a perfect fit with what you do, it provides an opportunity to trial a new area of work (such as during the start-up of your organisation), or is going to add additional areas to your work that you can potentially turn in to new products or services in the future.

The table below explains where social enterprise sits – between for profit businesses and charities, and the typical differences.

For Profit Business	Social Enterprise	Charity
Income from trading	Mix of income from trading, contracts, grants, fundraising & donations	Donations & Fundraising
Staff	Staff & Volunteers	Volunteers
Profit driven	Mix of social & financial returns	Not for profit Charitable purpose
Profits paid out to owners	Surpluses reinvested to support the social purpose &	Surpluses reinvested to support the charity's

	may be able to pay out some surpluses to investors/owners	mission
Reports on financial performance	Reports on social value and financial performance	Reports on public benefit, achievement of mission and financial performance

Business like attitude

So to be a social entrepreneur you need a business-like approach, some business sense, a determination to generate income and surpluses, and a passion to make a difference in the world. You need to be able to look at the world through different lenses and stick with your ideas. What you want to innovate and change may be laughed at by the hard-core commercially minded businessman, but if you get your social enterprise right, you will have greater riches than money can provide, and you will love going to work every day.

I have come across a lot of social entrepreneurs that do not approach their social enterprise with a business like attitude and treat it more like a hobby. As a consequence, the social enterprises, in most cases ceased to exist. Whatever you do, be passionate, but be professional at the same time.

The leader behind the social enterprise

Every social enterprise has a visionary leader – the person who wanted to set up the social enterprise in the first place, and without whom there would be no social enterprise. This person is the key to the future success or failure of the social enterprise – because their passion will either encourage others or scare them.

The visionary leader needs to find a way to make it happen and bring other people along on that journey with them. This can be particularly difficult if your background is practitioner based and you are not used to selling or marketing yourself and your ideas. In reality people buy from people they like and can connect with, so you have to be credible, believable, passionate and able to persuade funders, commissioners, members of the community, other organisations and your customers that they need to work with you and buy from you.

Another myth is that you can't have a wage from a social enterprise – or if you do it's a minimum wage that means you can't actually afford to live. A key rule of business – always pay yourself first. In a social enterprise this means making sure you are making money so you can pay yourself, otherwise you are effectively a volunteer. There are so many people that have a great idea and also say they are not interested in making any money, and of all the social enterprises I have worked with, these are the ones that have failed and closed within 2-3 years because the person needs to get a job elsewhere to pay their own bills! Once you are in this position you don't have the time, energy or focus to run your social enterprise effectively.

Why social enterprise now?

Social enterprise is a sector that is seeing huge growth globally because more people are becoming socially conscious. There are more people than ever who want to do something that will have an impact on people and the planet, as well as generate financial surpluses. More consumers are making ethical and conscious choices when buying, and supporting social enterprises. Now really is the time to join in the social enterprise revolution.

KEY POINTS

- A social enterprise is a way of doing business rather than a specific legal structure.
- You need to have a way to make money rather than depending on grant funding.
- You have to be business like.
- You have to be clear about your vision and share it.

Chapter 2: Deciding what your social enterprise will do

Follow your passion

When you make the decision to set up a social enterprise it is not the same as deciding to set up a for profit or commercial business. Your choice to have a social enterprise is driven by a deeper reason or passion, something you want to change in the world or a legacy you want to leave behind.

For me, my social enterprise is about incorporating my passion and skills. I love the concept of Ikigai – which is a Japanese concept that translates to "your reason for being". To me, this is what social enterprise is about. It's the reason you exist with such passion.

The diagram overleaf shows that your Ikigai sits at the centre of four overlapping areas:

1. Your passion – that which you love.
2. Your profession – that which you are good at without trying.
3. Something the world needs – that which frustrates you and you want to change in the world.

4. Your vocation – that which you can be paid for.

When you combine all four areas you are truly focused on your reason for being. Often people have four separate parts to their life, but Ikigai is about merging all four. How this has influenced me is that instead of:

- Being passionate about my son and helping children
- Having a profession as an Accountant
- Wanting to get rid of poverty in the world and
- Being paid to help social enterprises

I was able to combine the four things, so I now run and work with social enterprises that are supporting children and working to end poverty, using my financial and social enterprise skills. As part of what I do my son is a big part as he provides inspiration and ideas for my blogs and articles about finance, and the charity I have set up to support 100,000 children out of poverty is named after him.

There are other ways to identify and decide what your social enterprise could be set up for, including:

- Identifying a gap in the market
- New services the public sector are commissioning rather than continuing to deliver them internally
- A response to an event or issue in the community – such as a flood, fire, gun crime, lack of activities for young people, riots etc.

- Facing redundancy and wanting to continue the same type of activities
- Closure of existing local services

But whatever you do, you have to have a big enough Why. Why do you want to set up a social enterprise rather than a normal business? Often this question is met with the answer to access grants and funding. To me that is not a big enough reason, because it's actually harder to get grants than it is to trade.

Case study: Sociability Care CIC

Sociability Care CIC is an example of someone deciding to follow their passion. Jo-Anne Fisher set up the organisation in 2016. Here Jo-Anne explains why: For many years I dreamed of setting up Sociability Care but felt I needed to be in full time employment as I was reliant on a regular guaranteed salary each month.

However, in July 2015 my life changed forever. My twin boys, Oscar and Noah, were born 15 weeks early. Unfortunately our beautiful Noah only lived for 30 hours. Oscar spent the first 12 weeks of his life in hospital fighting for his life.

As a family we faced so many challenges and at a number of points we thought Oscar wouldn't be coming home. In October 2015 Oscar came home. Oscar has a variety of health difficulties including chronic lung disease, reflux, and he has cerebral palsy as he suffered a stroke when he was three days old. However he is our perfect boy. The birth of my sons made me realise it's NOW I want to develop Sociability Care. I want to utilise my skills and experience, make my boys proud and support other families in difficult situations.

I decided to set up a CIC because I wanted to involve both of my passions of supporting individuals with disabilities and their families (social) and delivering training to organisations (business). Having a CIC as a business model enables me to do that.

I think personally the most difficult part of setting up and running Sociability Care has been time. I've found I am constantly juggling all the different aspects of running a social enterprise on my own from building a website to finding funding. My journey has been a very steep learning curve.

To help start and develop Sociability Care I applied for the Lloyds Bank Social Entrepreneurs Programme which includes a 12 month business support programme and a £4,000 grant, and was successful. I have since applied for two grants and I am awaiting the outcome. I have found the grant application very time consuming and complex. As a result I have recently attended a free grant workshop to help develop my skills within this area.

I would like to see Sociability Care grow with the support of staff and volunteers to enable us to:

- support more individuals with disabilities and their families;
- support services within the community to be more inclusive and accessible; and
- have a strong presence in the community to continue to challenge and change peoples' attitudes towards disability.

I'd like us to be able to offer further services and have premises which can be accessed by the individuals we are working with. I think the key advice I would offer to all new and existing social enterprises is to work in partnership with other individuals and organisations. I think working together, sharing skills and ideas is the key to being successful.

Sociability Care aims to support individuals with disabilities and their families. We aim to reduce feelings of social isolation, promote independence and develop skills.

We provide training and guidance to organisations to ensure that services are inclusive and confident in meeting the needs of the organisation's user group. It ensures that the service is delivered to all users by an experienced, motivated and confident workforce.

www.sociabilitycare.org

www.facebook.com/sociabilitycare/

Deciding what you love

Another way to decide what your social enterprise will do is to focus on what you love and how you want to feel every day. To work out what that means for you I always say to people to find three words that describe how you want to feel every day.

Once you have these three words you make decisions every day based on whether what you are about to do gives you one of those three words. For me, last year, my three words were peace, learning and appreciation.

Equipped with these words I could then very easily decide if I wanted to do a piece of consultancy work from the perspective of whether it would bring learning or appreciation in to my life, rather than just thinking from a financial perspective. As peace was my other word, having time to spend in my garden was important, as well as working from home to avoid the stressful daily commute to work.

By applying this test to everything:

- You have more time because you are saying no to what you don't want, and you are comfortable saying no because it doesn't create one of your three feelings.
- People respect you more because you have started to respect yourself and put your needs first.
- You have more energy and can achieve more because you love what you are doing.

This approach works perfectly for your social enterprise, as well as in life in general, because you can decide which activities, projects, services, products etc. fit with your three words. As you will be leading the organisation it's important that whatever it is doing is something you are passionate about, love doing and enjoy.

Creating a vision and mission statement

Once you have decided what your social enterprise will do it's a good idea to write out your vision and mission statements. Vision and mission statements are short sentences stating your organisation's purpose and why it exists (your mission), and the change you are seeking or how you want the world to look (your vision).

Examples of Vision and Mission statements include:

Cysters - Mission: "Our mission is to reduce the social stigma attached with women's gynae health, through education, awareness and campaigning further research."

Start Again Project – Mission: "Start Again's Mission is for young people to develop their personal, spiritual and social development. Enabling them to lead a fuller life in their communities."

ChangeKitchen – Mission: "ChangeKitchen's mission is to be part of a revolution that turns access to healthy eating away from a privilege to a right for everyone."

Oxfam – Mission: "Our purpose is to help create lasting solutions to the injustice of poverty. We are part of a global movement for change, empowering people to create a future that is secure, just, and free from poverty."

Oxfam – Vision: "Our vision is a just world without poverty. We want a world where people are valued and treated equally, enjoy their rights as full citizens, and can influence decisions affecting their lives."

Lewis Enterprise Foundation – Vision: "Our vision is a world where children have positive futures and opportunities."

KEY POINTS

- Get clear on what your own passions are.
- Combine your skills, experiences and passions to bring about change.
- Create vision and mission statements that concisely describe your organisation's purpose and the change you want to see.

CHAPTER 3: DEVELOPING THE BUSINESS IDEA

Creating a business plan

Once you have identified your idea the next stage is to develop this further by creating a business plan. There are a number of options available for creating a business plan, and there are free templates available online. I prefer short, concise business plans so I recommend using the Social Business Model Canvas which is a way to create a business plan on one sheet of paper. It covers everything that would go in a traditional business plan but it is much more concise, and it is a great way to get your ideas down on paper quickly. You can then expand this and incorporate it in a more formal business plan.

Why bother with a business plan?

A business plan is really just evidence that you have thought about how you are going to develop your social enterprise, and that you are serious about it. Often funders or investors will ask for your business plan when you apply to them if you are asking for funding or investment for more than one year. Funders will be looking to see that your organisation can be sustainable and won't be dependent on funding forever (so you would need to show a growth in other sources of income such as trading), and investors will be interested in whether you can pay the investment back (so they will be looking at the income figures you are presenting and also the surpluses you intend to generate).

The more obvious and common reason for having a business plan is so you know what you are doing. It will set out your goals and plans for the organisation, and break these down in to targets for the next three years or five years. This will include targets for things like:

- Your vision and mission
- Your legal structure
- Who your beneficiaries/clients are
- Number of beneficiaries/clients you will work with
- Outcomes you will achieve
- Income amount and where this will come from
- Expenditure breakdown including key items of expense
- Any investment or cashflow requirements and potential sources of this
- Surpluses you intend to have
- What services/products you are offering
- Where you offer those products/services
- What the marketplace/sector looks like and any potential opportunities

- How you will operate your organisation
- What management and staff team you will have
- What your Board looks like and the skills they have
- Who you work in partnership with
- How you market your organisation
- What reputation and values your organisation will have
- The future vision for the organisation

For many social entrepreneurs preparing a business plan is a daunting and difficult process because they have never done anything like this before. But do not become discouraged. Access free support that is available to help with this –through your local voluntary services council or social enterprise support agencies. These organisations typically have European or Local Authority funded contracts to provide free support to social enterprise start ups, which usually includes help with business plans, access to free training and other support.

From my own experience I have met a lot of social entrepreneurs who have the business plan in their head, and have never written anything down on paper. I have done this myself as well in the past, but what I have learnt is that when you write something down it becomes a goal. When it is in your head it is more like a dream. For a couple of years with my own organisation I didn't update my business plan and guess what? My organisation barely grew, no new services were developed and there was nothing to link objectives for staff to. The next year when I did update the business plan and link the staff objectives to achieving the goals and financial targets the organisation nearly doubled in size.

My tips for business planning are:

- Make this a living document that is reviewed regularly and used to set your monthly and quarterly goals, rather than writing it and then only looking at it once a year.
- Have specific targets and goals that are allocated to particular individuals with timescales for completion, as well as regular reviews of progress. Without this no-one is accountable for achieving the plans in the business plan.
- Make sure you have researched your market sector properly and know what you are talking about. If you are not sure contact someone who has the relevant expertise to get the information you require.
- Don't ignore the financial information – often people leave this section, but without the financial forecasts it is impossible to see if the organisation will be viable and worth setting up. And without any financial

targets and goals linked to your plans you won't know if you are achieving what you set out to do.

- Be realistic – don't overestimate the income, surpluses, number of people you will work with or the social impact you will have. Also be realistic about the resources and time you have available.
- Think about who your audience is (your Board/Management team, investors, funders etc.) and write the business plan accordingly.
- Have a strong management team/Board supporting the development of the organisation. Initially it may just be you but think about who else could support you by being on your Board or acting in an advisory role so you have access to expertise in different areas. It will make your business plan more credible if you have involved the right people.
- Get someone to review your business plan to check it makes sense, is consistent and also is not under or over stating things.

KEY POINTS

- Develop a business plan so you have clear targets and goals.
- Incorporate the financial information in the plan.

- Get help and support with this if you need it and get the plan reviewed by someone independent.
- Regularly review and update the plan, and use it to make sure you keep on track with your various goals.

Further information:

The Social Business Model Canvas template and guidance: www.socialbusinessmodelcanvas.com

Guidance on business planning and links to business plan template and the financial templates: https://www.gov.uk/write-business-plan and www.startuploans.co.uk/business-planning-templates

Free support with developing your social enterprise idea: www.the-sse.org and www.unltd.org.uk

CHAPTER 4: STAYING BALANCED AND AVOIDING BURNOUT

Tired and frustrated?

As the social entrepreneur who had the vision and desire to set up a social enterprise you have a vested interest in the success of the organisation. This can often mean you work to the point of exhaustion and take on too much because you have such a desire to do more social good and grow your organisation. You probably imagined running a social enterprise as something very fulfilling and rewarding, that was always exciting, but the reality can be very different – working long hours without any support or help.

This can mean you become burnt out, stressed, frustrated or too tired to focus clearly. All of these things can lead to mistakes, making the wrong decisions and not being able to achieve what you hoped for. It's also very likely that at the beginning you will take on lots of different roles in the organisation (including marketing, networking, posting on social media, developing the website, sorting out IT problems, financial management, cleaning, making the tea, answering the phone, delivering the services/products and trying to develop the organisation at the same time), and often these will take you a long time as you are learning new skills, or simply muddling your way through.

Working long hours

One of the big risks when setting up and running a social enterprise is that you become exhausted and worn out from working too hard. Having experienced this myself, when I used to work 14-15 hours a day, often six days a week, and where I eventually became ill, I want to share some tips for ensuring you maximise the use of your time.

From my personal experience, I changed my working life completely, and now I work two days a week and have more impact and make more money than when I was working six days a week. It's all about focus and efficiency, and recognising the things you are good at and not wasting your time and energy doing things you aren't very good at.

Work on your organisation NOT in it

This phrase about working on your organisation rather than in it, is said a lot these days – but it holds true. If you are spending all your time responding to emails, telephone calls and operational issues, your organisation can't and won't grow.

It's also very easy for me to say, stop working in your organisation, but the reality is until you completely review and change your daily schedule this isn't going to happen. This is also something that needs to happen naturally as you grow the organisation, and is something to phase in as other people take responsibility for some of the things you have been doing. A simple step you can take now is to think about what you need to stop doing. Ask yourself, "What do I need to STOP doing?" Think about:

- What is not working?
- What leaves you feeling frustrated and stressed?
- What doesn't add any value to your organisation?
- What is not your area of expertise?

Write them down on a 'Stop Doing List' and then develop a plan to stop doing these items with timescales.

By setting aside time to work on your organisation, you will be able to:

- Develop new products/services
- Innovate
- Network
- Identify new partners and joint ventures

- Identify potential customers and connect with them
- Think strategically about the future of your organisation
- Have clear long term goals and plans

Get clear on your goals and work on them

Everyone has goals, but often these aren't very clear. For example, you want to increase your organisation's income or you want to work with more people, but you haven't stated how you will do this, when you will do it by, or how much you want to increase these things by. By breaking it down to weekly and daily targets these are much more manageable and achievable, and more likely to actually be done rather than forgotten about.

How can you grow your organisation?

Is it about generating more customers, creating new products or services, partnering or doing a joint venture with another organisation, promoting yourself through key networks and individuals, or buying or merging with another organisation, or something else? Think about the opportunities available to you that can achieve what you desire for your social enterprise in the quickest and easiest way, so you don't become exhausted.

Take back control of your day

Rather than letting your day run you, decide what you will do each day. I used to have days where I would plan to develop a new service, but instead I would get emails, calls and requests from clients throughout the day, and I ran out of time to develop that new service. Now, I set aside three hours at least once a week to work strategically on my organisation. During this time I don't take phone calls or respond to emails. I focus entirely on actions that will help to grow my organisation. I also block out time for responding to emails and telephone calls, and this is usually mid morning and mid afternoon. Also, think about what you can delegate or get other people to help you with.

Get a morning routine

One of the quickest and easiest ways to transform your organisation and the productivity of your day is to establish a routine each morning. My routine consists of meditating for 15 minutes after I have dropped my son at nursery. Then I prioritise the tasks I have for the day. Before I start any of these tasks on my to do list, I spend 15-20 minutes doing three things that will generate income for my organisation.

This is a really easy way to make sure you achieve something each day. My three things typically include posting details of events or services on social media, contacting someone to speak at their event, calling a customer for payment, scoping a new product or service, or recording a short promotional video. Make this a habit, so you do this every morning. Don't do anything else until you have done your three things.

Look at what you are naturally pre-disposed to enjoy doing

I recently did The Vitality Test, which helps you identify your natural state, and the way you tend to function. TheVitalityTest.com was created by Nicholas Haines and looks at your balance of the five energies the Chinese discovered over 3,000 years ago - Water, Wood, Fire, Earth and Metal. Based on your balance between these you are pre-disposed to be good at certain things. The test is free to take and you receive a report detailing what your results mean.

In my case I have high wood and metal energies. This means I like to continually innovate and have lots of ideas, and that I am also someone who likes to complete things. For me this is a good balance because I can take lots of the ideas I have and actually complete them. If I didn't have high metal energy then I would probably have lots of ideas but never complete them – which is typical of a lot of entrepreneurs. If you are like that you would need someone who is a completer to help you get your organisation beyond just an idea.

Get clarity on your beliefs around work

Everybody has beliefs about work. A lot of people believe you have to be employed and that having your own business is risky. Through the work I have done with social entrepreneurs I know many of them have beliefs about how they should earn their money, and also about having to do everything themselves to the point of being exhausted.

The other big issue many social entrepreneurs have is around their income ceiling. This is the maximum amount of money you feel comfortable earning. The problem if this is too low is that you will struggle to get more than this level of income in your social enterprise. If you have ever experienced sudden financial setback, had difficulty generating income no matter how hard you try, or wondered why you can't seem to get ahead then you most likely have a belief around your income ceiling. This means you will do everything possible to maintain the status quo of your current income level – a depressing thought if you are trying to grow your organisation.

Your beliefs control how you function on a daily basis – over 80% of your actions each day are subconscious based on your beliefs and the programmes you run. This makes it very difficult to change your thoughts and your behaviour unless you change your beliefs. By getting clear on your beliefs and blocks around work and income you can identify why your social enterprise isn't growing. Spend some time focusing on the language you use when you talk about your organisation and its finances. Then make a conscious effort to change this to more positive language in order to achieve what you desire with your organisation.

That difficult person

Inevitably, at some point on your journey you will meet someone who says your idea is rubbish, you aren't the right person to set up the social enterprise, you don't know what you are talking about or who simply won't give you the funding or contract you want. You have two options – either give up and believe what they are saying, or go round this person, stay focused on what you want and keep moving forward.

I remember, about 12 years ago, an organisation I was working with wanted to get the support of a very prominent individual in the local area. This person was able to say which organisations should get the local authority funding and without their support it was well known organisations would struggle to succeed. But this person was not happy that someone had an idea to work in the community that had not been identified by them, and they refused to support the organisation. The lead person in the organisation decided to work to connect strategically with individuals higher up in the local authority and as a result secured local authority funding from another pot of money. Not everyone you meet is going to support you, but it doesn't mean you can't achieve what you planned.

KEY POINTS

- Focus on working ON not IN your organisation.
- To avoid tiredness and exhaustion create a Stop Doing List.
- Get clear on your goals and take control of your day.
- Develop a morning routine.
- Identify your natural talents and beliefs and work to build on these.

Further information:

Setting goals and being efficient: The 12 Week Year Book by Brian P. Moran and Michael Lennington

CHAPTER 5: SETTING UP A SOCIAL ENTERPRISE

Legal structure options

When it comes to setting up a social enterprise there are a number of different legal structures available to you. Social enterprises can be any legal structure. I firmly believe that social enterprise is not restricted to a particular form of legal structure.

Some will argue as to whether a sole trader could be a social enterprise, but I believe they can be – because social enterprise is about the way you do business not your legal structure. You can be a window cleaner that uses the profits to provide social events for the elderly – that's a social enterprise!

The legal structures available are: sole trader, partnership, limited company, Community Interest Company, charity, Charitable Incorporated Organisation, Community Benefit Society, Charitable Community Benefit Society and Co-operative Society.

So how do you decide which legal structure is right? This section details the key points regarding each legal structure. Although the process of getting your legal structure officially set up can often take a long time, it is actually the easiest part of the process of establishing a social enterprise.

Sole trader

This is simply being self-employed. You prepare a personal tax return and pay tax and NIC on the profits you generate. You are your business, and unlike most of the other legal structures there is no separate legal entity, so if your business is sued you as an individual are liable.

Partnership

Very few social enterprises use this structure, but it is ideal where two individuals or organisations wish to work together. A Limited Liability Partnership provides the partnership with a separate legal entity as well, so the partners cannot be sued.

Limited Company

Here you have a choice between limited by share and limited by guarantee. Most large voluntary organisations that are not charitable companies are set up as limited by guarantee companies. In this situation you have members and a Board, but no shares or shareholders, so no dividends can be paid. Care should be taken if you set up a limited by guarantee company and are not registered with

Charity Commission where you have charitable objects. It is a legal requirement to register with them once your income is above £5,000. To avoid this you will need to have objects that are not charitable.

A limited by share company is the standard structure for most commercial businesses, and is not usually seen as being a structure for a social enterprise because all the profits can be paid to the shareholders via dividends. I have seen exceptions to this, where the Articles of Association have been amended to limit the dividends that can be paid to shareholders (which is similar to taking on some of the characteristics of a Community Interest Company).

Community Interest Company (CIC)

This is one of the most common legal structures for social enterprises because it requires the company to have a community benefit. It also has an asset lock which prevents assets being sold at undervalue and requires the CIC to use its assets for its designated community benefit. CICs are required to report annually on how they have delivered their community benefit, but the governance is much lighter than with a charity. A CIC enables the entrepreneur to receive a wage through the company, and also retain control over decision making as a director. If the CIC is limited by share the shareholders can receive a dividend up to a maximum of 35% of the profits.

Case study: Cysters CIC

Cysters CIC is a perfect example of the benefits of setting up a CIC. Neelam Heera, the founder of Cysters explains why she set up Cysters and chose a CIC legal structure:

I set this group up following my own difficulty with gynaecological issues. I also have a full time job so I wanted to set this social enterprise up in the background whilst being able to fund myself. Due to having a full time job I wouldn't be able to satisfy the criteria to set up a charity so the community aspect of a social enterprise worked well for me.

The lack of resources available to start-ups has been difficult for me. Juggling working and not having someone on hand to assist me through the setup has been difficult, particularly as I'm not accustomed to business planning. I would advise anyone to be organised. I have found this to be my downfall and my lack of organisation had led me to become behind and scatty in my initial approach to this business model.

In ten years' time I hope that Cysters will have grown across the United Kingdom and become the leading company specialising in gynaecological awareness, support and research.

Cysters' ethos is to make sure that all women, no matter their background, feel they have support in a confidential environment.

Cysters aims to:

- Bring awareness of gynaecological health such as Polycystic Ovary Syndrome (PCOS), Endometriosis, Infertility, Gynaecological Cancers, Female Genital Mutilation (FGM) and Menopause to the forefront.
- To reduce the social stigma in the BAME community regarding gynaecological health by educating people about these problems. Since starting this group I have noticed that it is still a cultural taboo to talk about gynaecological problems.
- To provide support for women suffering with these issues through group sessions covering topics such as body confidence etc.

www.cysters.co.uk

@cystersbham

@neelamheera

www.facebook.com/cystersbham

Charity

A charity can be unincorporated, which means the trustees are personally liable if anything goes wrong with the charity. This type of charity has a constitution which sets out its purpose (objects) and the rules for how it will operate.

If you decide to have a charitable company, it will be registered with both Charity Commission and Companies House, and there will be requirements to file annual returns and accounts with both of these. The main benefit of a charitable company is that trustees are not personally liable. Governance of charities is much more restrictive than other types of legal structures and there are restrictions on the number of trustees that can receive payment from the charity. Generally, it is not seen as good practice for the Chief Executive (who is salaried) to also be a trustee. For this reason, many entrepreneurs work in the charity but give away control to their Board of trustees.

Charities must be registered with Charity Commission once their income reaches £5,000. Below this level you can apply to HMRC for recognition as a charity for tax purposes.

Charitable Incorporated Organisation (CIO)

A CIO provides the benefits of a charitable company type structure without the requirement to be registered with Companies House. This means all filing and monitoring is carried out by Charity Commission, and the CIO is just subject to Charity Law and not Company Law as well.

Community Benefit Society

A Community Benefit Society (CBS) is set up to benefit the community and like a CIC has an asset lock to ensure the assets are only used for the community. A CBS is expected to trade or run a business for the benefit of the community and has members who own shares in the CBS. The shares are withdrawable shares (so they cannot be sold or transferred to another person, but would be given back to the CBS at the price the share was purchased for). The members cannot receive a share of any of the profits.

Charitable Community Benefit Society (CCBS)

A CCBS is a CBS that is also a charity. This requires the CCBS to exclusively operate and trade to achieve its charitable purpose and objects. A CCBS is not registered with Charity Commission, but applies to HMRC to be recognised as an exempt charity for tax purposes. A CCBS can issue withdrawable shares to its members and pay interest on the shares. A CCBS must have an asset lock in place.

Co-operative Society

The key distinctive parts of a Co-operative society are that member participation and involvement is crucial, and that the society is set up to serve the interests of its members. There is no requirement to have an asset lock, although the Co-operative society can have a voluntary asset lock. The society can pay dividends to its member based on their transactions with the Co-operative Society.

The International Co-operative Alliance's statement on the Co-operative Identity, Values and Principles, defines a co-operative as "an autonomous association of persons united voluntarily to meet their common economic, social, and cultural needs and aspirations through a jointly owned and democratically controlled enterprise." A Co-operative society can be set up with any legal structure as long as it meets the principles and values included in the International Co-operative Alliance's Statement on the Co-operative Identity, Values and Principles.

Special Status and Hybrids

In addition to this you can choose to have special status, such as a Community Amateur Sports Club or Enterprise Development Agency and each of these offers additional benefits or tax reliefs, in addition to those you obtain with your legal structure.

You can also have combinations of structures – such as a CIC Co-op – which is legally structured as a CIC but has many of the features of a Co-op because it is a membership organisation.

Deciding which legal structure to adopt

Typically, the decision regarding which legal structure to operate your social enterprise through is largely down to the awareness of the entrepreneur about different legal structures and also whether that legal structure is eligible for the type of income or finance you are planning to have.

What works?

The majority of social enterprises I have worked with have been CICs Limited by Guarantee. This structure appeals to the solo entrepreneur as they can operate as a social enterprise without losing control of the organisation or having extensive governance in place.

My top tips for choosing a legal structure are:

- Make an informed choice – talk to people who have a social enterprise with the legal structure you are considering, and ask them what the pros and cons are.
- Don't rely solely on a professional advisor or consultant to tell you what legal structure to have – because this may be driven by their awareness of, or preference for, a particular structure.
- Consider the longer term goals and plans you have for the social enterprise, and also your personal goals, to make sure the legal structure will still be fit for purpose in 5, 10 or 15 years.
- Be aware of the tax and regulatory implications of your choice, rather than finding out about them later.

What if you choose the wrong legal structure?

Personally I have found that the process of changing legal structure is not always an ideal thing to do – particularly if you cannot convert your existing legal structure to the new structure you require, as this results in setting up a new organisation with no track record, trading history or accounts. This means it is important to weigh up the pros and cons of each legal structure, and also to be clear about what you will require in 3, 5 and even 10 years' time if possible to avoid having to change your legal structure.

If you do set up and then decide you have the wrong legal structure, it is better to change it sooner rather than later, as there will be less to transfer and less track record that is potentially lost.

Case Study: Our Sorority

Our Sorority is an example of an organisation that changed its legal structure during the early stages of its existence. Alicia Barnes, the Chief Executive Officer of Our Sorority, explains, "I set up a CIC limited by guarantee initially as I had experience in managing a CIC previously, and I knew that the registration process was straight forward and easy to do. I thought that my organisation would be making a substantial profit on some of the work that we were doing and assumed that being a CIC was the right route to take for the organisation.

I decided to change into a registered charity (CIO) as I found that I would not be making too much profit from the programmes that I deliver as I would receive grants for this work and funding was easier for me to source as a registered charity to support the organisation.

49

A lot of people do not know or understand what a CIC is so when explaining that it is social enterprise which uses profits to benefit the community it caused a lot of confusion to people who were not in this sector as it sounded much like a charity. I feel that charities get more recognition than CICs.

The benefits of being a CIC were that the filing and reporting process was much easier and straight forward. However, the benefits of being a charity are greater. Even though the reporting process is a bit more complicated, the benefits of being a charity for us is greater as:

- We have access to more sources of funding
- We receive more recognition as a charity
- A lot more people understand what a charity is so we get more donations and support from the community
- We have better governance as a charity due to us having trustees
- We can get tax relief (gift aid) on donations

I found the process of setting up the CIC quite easy. Setting up the charity was difficult for me as I had to research how to convert the CIC, only to find out that I had to dissolve the CIC to make the CIO. I tried completing the charity application myself which was rejected as it was not completed in the correct way. I then had to pay a large amount of money for a solicitor who said that they specialised in this to complete the application. Their first application was rejected and had to be completed again. This process took over six months to complete.

Our Sorority act as an advocate for young women aged 15-25 to empower and support them with their personal, professional and parental development. This will enable them to develop and maintain a positive way of life. We do this by giving guidance and practical support to vulnerable young women who are (but not limited to) at risk of offending, abuse, substance misuse, poverty, exploitation, child protection orders, managing their mental health, NEET and who feel excluded from society.

We have a holistic approach in supporting them with their personal, professional and parental development. Our Sorority provides a wide range of skills and practical support through mentoring, workshops and family support.

www.oursorority.co.uk

@Oursorority1

Instagram: Oursorority_charity

www.facebook.com/Oursorority

KEY POINTS

- Research the different legal structures.
- Weigh up the financial and tax benefits of each structure, alongside the governance requirements.
- Choose a structure that is suitable for now as well as 3, 5 and 10 years' time.

Further information:

For a full list of pros and cons of each legal structure please check out Unltd's Legal Help Guide: Structures for Social Enterprise.

Most regulatory bodies provide template or model Articles or Constitutions. These model documents are suitable for social enterprises in the majority of cases, unless you wish to have more complex governing arrangements, such as a range of members, owners and investors, or need to add in additional clauses. Please refer to the following websites:

Charity Commission:
www.gov.uk/government/organisations/charity-commission

Companies House:
www.gov.uk/government/organisations/companies-house

CIC Regulator:
www.gov.uk/government/organisations/office-of-the-regulator-of-community-interest-companies

CBS & Co-operatives:
www.fca.org.uk/firms/mutual-societies

Co-operatives UK: http://www.uk.coop/

SECTION TWO

CHAPTER 6: CLARITY REGARDING YOUR PRODUCTS AND SERVICES

The importance of products and services

Often when individuals decide they want to set up a social enterprise it is to make a difference or create change in society. Many expect that because they are doing something good for society they will get funding. This is not always the case, and increasingly grant funded social enterprises are struggling to survive. This is why having a set of products or services that you can sell puts you in a stronger position. This does not detract or reduce your social purpose, it supports you to deliver more of it – as you have income and surpluses to enable you to do more of your good work. If you want to be around in 10 years' time and not continually chasing grant funding, then developing a range of products and services is your best option.

What are products and services?

Products and services are simply anything that you deliver or provide as an organisation.

So how do you decide what products or services you should deliver?

I frequently refer to the Income Mix – or the marriage made in heaven, where you have a beautiful three tier wedding cake.

In order to minimise risk and dependency in terms of income sources you need to have three tiers to your income:

- a mix of products or services
- a mix of customers, and
- a mix of income types.

Which products or services to sell?

The process I take clients through when helping them to identify their products or services is:

- Who are your clients?
- What do you currently deliver for those clients?
- What are you good at? What are your strengths and what is unique to your organisation?
- What needs do your clients have that you currently don't meet?
- How could you address those needs? Are there opportunities for developing new products or services?
- Does this align with your social purpose?
- Who would buy the product or service? This is an important question to ask if you usually

offer your services or products for free to the end user.

I recommend a minimum of three different products or services so you are not dependent on any one item for your income. Products or services can be packages, or alternatively split into different items, as well as having different levels of each item (such as bronze, silver and gold versions).

Case Study: Start Again Project CIC

Start Again Project CIC is an example of an organisation that looked at what other areas of support its beneficiaries needed, and moved in to that area of support. Here Mark Peters, the founder and CEO shares the story:

I was frustrated that my mentally ill brother's needs were not being properly met, so I decided to do something about it. I created Start Again, a project that uses football sessions to address the lack of support available to young people suffering from mental health issues.

Initially Start Again provided outreach sports and wellbeing programmes, mainly through football to young people at risk of, or with, mental health issues. The sessions provided access to a structured, safe and enabling environment with football as a hook into a wide range of developmental services.

I wanted to take our work a step further and housing was one of the biggest issues faced by the young people we worked with. Often their relationships with their family have broken down and they need to live elsewhere. We had referred young people to housing providers so they could move in to supported accommodation, but it often wasn't successful because the accommodation or support were not appropriate.

This made me realise that Start Again needed to have its own accommodation for the young people we were working with. We secured a Big Lottery Fund grant to develop a house with supported accommodation. We were then lucky to see an opportunity to tender to the Empty Homes Fund – to provide funding to refurbish empty properties in Birmingham so they could be let out. We were successful in receiving this funding, and refurbished eight properties.

At the time all our income was grants and for delivering activities. It was a continual process of chasing the next piece of grant funding. Now, four years since we started providing supported accommodation services for young people the majority of our income is from the accommodation. We have much more certainty in terms of our income providing the houses are occupied, and the grant income continues to provide the wellbeing and activities to support these young people. It means the organisation is in a much stronger financial position, and our income has grown rapidly over the past four years.

Looking back, it was partly luck and also taking the opportunity to enter a new area of work that would help the young people we were already working with. At the time I didn't realise how much providing accommodation would change Start Again.

Start Again Project is set up to enable young people to lead full lives in their communities. Start Again enables young people to develop understanding and skills this will allow them to:

- Build confidence to broaden horizons
- Socialise and have fun
- Inspire young people to set their own goals
- To provide relevant and appropriate opportunities to young people
- Promote healthy living
- Provide safe homes and stability

info@start-again.co.uk

www.start-again.co.uk

www.facebook.com/StartAgainProjectCIC

@startagaincic

The right mix of customers

I have seen a lot of organisations chase grant funding, and try to fit what they do in to a funder's criteria or worse change what they do to fit in to it – and in the process lose sight of why the organisation was set up and have mission drift – where the organisation drifts away from its original mission or purpose and starts working with different beneficiary groups. To avoid this, you need to be clear about what products, services and activities you provide and stick to what you are good at. It is acceptable to add additional items where these link to your existing services and where there is a need from the clients you work with. For example, if you currently provide mentoring and through delivering this you find that a lot of your clients also need help with drug or alcohol issues you may decide to expand in to this area. A not so great example, if you currently work with young people and a contract comes out to work with the elderly, and you decide to tender because you need the income – but you have no experience in this area of work.

I have also seen organisations develop products and services that are targeting a different customer/client because they aren't the same as what they currently offer. As this is risky it is better to put this in a separate organisation or company in case anything goes wrong. For example, I worked with a youth based educational charity and they decided to set up a social enterprise hairdressers to train young people to be hairdressers. As their core services weren't hairdressing they set this up through a separate CIC.

There are a number of ways to identify your customers – if you are trading directly with the public or businesses, then it is a case of getting really clear on the issues you solve for these customers. Identify the niche you want to work with and get specific – who is your perfect customer? When I set up my social enterprise accountancy business I would often get asked by other accountants if I could get enough business by just working with charities and social enterprises, because they believed you also had to work with small businesses. When I said 85% of the clients were social enterprises, around 10% self employed and 5% for profit companies they always seemed shocked, but I had defined my niche and become a specialist in that area which generated new leads and clients automatically. To get to that place you have to be specific and get known as the go to organisation for that customer group.

If you are planning on obtaining funding or contracts you will have two customers. The end beneficiaries and the person paying for the products/services. But you still need to be clear about who your perfect customer is – so identify the commissioners and foundations/trusts that will fund what you do, and also identify who your beneficiaries are.

A mix of income sources

Lots of organisations are dependent on one main funder that provides around 80-90% of their income over a three year period. Towards the end of year 3 the panic sets in and the organisation goes into meltdown as they try to find a new source of income to continue to exist or get a continuation of their existing funding/contract. If you are ever in the position to secure a grant that can cover all your running costs and core staff posts don't wait until year three to start developing other income sources, start looking for these straightaway. Your organisation is high risk if you don't have several different customers/funders and income sources.

By doing this process you may find that there aren't many commissioners or funders interested in what you do. So, you will need to get a plan b – where can you generate income from? Your potential options are:

- Charge your beneficiaries (see Chapter 7)
- Get donations from individuals or businesses
- Sponsorship from businesses
- Hold fundraising events

- Joint venture or partnership with existing organisations
- Become part of a consortia and be a sub-contractor delivering in your niche area
- Sell something to the general public or businesses to finance the activities you want to deliver
- Develop a franchise model and sell this to other organisations to deliver in other geographical locations

Ideally you want to have a mix of income sources – so you have grants, donations, sponsorship, contracts and trading income. If you solely trade, then it is vital that you have a range of customers rather than one or two large customers that are the bulk of your income and a range of products/services as well with no one product accounting for more than 40% of your income. Again, I have seen organisations with one customer (usually a statutory agency or local authority) and when they are hit with budget cuts they stop buying from the organisation and the organisation rarely survives the huge reduction in their income.

The only way to achieve a mix of income is to set yourself targets for spreading your income across these different sources. If you are 100% grant funded it is advisable to work towards achieving 20-30% of your income from other sources over 18 months.

If you are 100% trading and have one customer that accounts for more than 25% of your income, over 18 months I would work to reduce this to 10% of total income. Also, if you only have one product or service, again I would seek to introduce other products and services to reduce dependency on one item.

Case study: ChangeKitchen CIC

ChangeKitchen is a great example of partnership working. In this case study Birgit Kehrer, the founder and CEO shares details of the partnership ChangeKitchen has:

I was already working as a sole trader with social aims and wanted to expand – and as I never wanted to work 'just for profit', Social Enterprise was the obvious choice. I have always wanted to be involved in supporting change and with ChangeKitchen that is about supporting people back to work who otherwise find it hard to get extra chances.

I have been working in partnership with many different organisations – mostly very successfully. The social enterprise sector, big parts of the charity sector and other third sector organisations are great at working together and working towards aims together. Initially, ChangeKitchen was set up as a joint venture, but as we grew and I had a different vision for the future, that joint venture ended. I have also worked in partnership with other organisations, sharing premises etc.

I am currently working in joint venture with The Jericho Foundation (a charity supporting people back to work via the vehicle of a variety of social enterprises) – and am finding it greatly beneficial. I am told it equally benefits The Jericho Foundation working with us – so that's a win win situation. It helps ChangeKitchen as a smaller social enterprise to get support through the larger infrastructure and has really been beneficial for recent growth. The Jericho Foundation have helped us with premises, equipment, transportation, back office support such as doing our finances and with providing volunteers and staff.

The biggest issues I encountered was working with some charities where the board is clearly not yet embracing the entrepreneurial spirit and therefore struggles with buying into social enterprise being about 'enterprise' and not just 'social' – then issues like investment into the future and earning income can become complicated.

The one thing I have learnt from working in partnership and having joint ventures is that I would be more insistent to get certain partnership relationships put into words on paper to avoid problems. I would also make an even bigger effort to get external specialist support for anyone with particular issues working for ChangeKitchen. Working with people with multiple barriers can be difficult if you are – like me – a blue eyed enthusiast rather than an expert in certain issues.

In the future I am aiming to have more outlets in Birmingham, plus a freezer range in a variety of shops and a specialist social enterprise/ethical wedding package together.

My advice to anyone thinking about working in partnership or having a joint venture is to get good advice and support before you start and keep asking questions and for support once you get going.

ChangeKitchen CIC is a vegetarian and vegan event catering company specialising in high quality events with amazing food and excellent service. ChangeKitchen's mission is to be part of a revolution that turns access to healthy eating away from a privilege to a right for everyone. Our goals are simple:

- to meet a demand for catering that is delicious, nutritious and which supports a healthy lifestyle,
- to contribute to a local, sustainable and healthy food economy,
- to provide training and work opportunities to people who face social exclusion and

- to support them into mainstream employment and a more stable lifestyle.

www.changekitchen.co.uk

Twitter: @changekitchen

Instagram: @changekitchen

Facebook: ChangeKitchen

Consortia and Franchises

It is worth mentioning these briefly as possible ways to develop your income mix. Consortia are simply groups of organisations that work together and tender for larger contracts that they would not be eligible for individually. To me this is like partnership working, except you probably have 5-10 partners – all with different demands and requirements which can make it difficult to operate a consortium successfully.

Franchises are a way for you to package up your product or service, and provide a manual for other organisations to deliver the same thing in a different geographical area. One of the organisations I work with – Cancer United – are currently developing this type of model to create cancer support groups across the country.

KEY POINTS

- Identify what products and services you can provide.
- Be clear about who your customers are.
- Think about how you can have different types of income.
- Have a mix of products and services, a mix of customers, and a mix of income types to minimise dependency on any one of these.

Further information:

Partnership working: www.socialenterprise.org.uk (The Power of Partnerships: Partnership Toolkit)

Social franchising: www.socialenterprise.org.uk (Social Franchising Manual)

CHAPTER 7: PRICING YOUR PRODUCTS AND SERVICES

Pricing and selling versus Costing and giving

For me this is the biggest learning for most social enterprises - being able to move from basing everything on cost and breaking even - to looking at pricing and being financially viable.

Free services versus Getting people to pay

If you are planning on obtaining grants for your organisation I believe if at all possible people should pay for the services/products/activities they receive, even if that is only 50p or £1. Through the experience I have gained people do not value things that are free. Also, most funders will ask you how you intend to become sustainable after their grant funding has ended, so being able to generate some income towards the costs is positive.

Pricing your product or service

When I am delivering training I love to ask someone to say how much they want to earn each month from their social enterprise. Let's say, it's £3,000.

- If you charge £10 per item or hour you need to work 300 hours a month or produce 300 items a month.
- If you charge £100 then it's 30 hours or items.
- If you charge £1,000 then it's 3 hours or items.

When you add in the time you spend on marketing, networking, business development, staff development, training, finances etc, how many hours can you realistically be selling for? Make sure you include all this time to get to the true cost of your product or service. This process makes it much easier to work out how many of your products or services you need to sell each week, month and year to cover your costs.

This makes pricing a guaranteed area where social entrepreneurs get stuck. Especially because so many are just interested in the social, and forget without the right price there won't be sufficient money to achieve their social purpose.

Identifying your value

The value you deliver is all about the issues you solve for your customer – whether that is an individual, funder or commissioner. If you can give them what they want and need, you are solving a problem for them and in that process you become of value.

Most people totally undervalue their worth and the value of their product or service. A study carried out by Professor Poundstone (Priceless: The Myth of Fair Value) looked at purchasing patterns with beer and how the concept of value in the customer's eyes can be changed. In the first test, customers had to pick between a standard beer priced at £1.80 or a premium beer at £2.50. 80% selected the premium beer. In the second test, a third beer was added that was priced at £1.60. In this scenario, 80% bought the £1.80 beer, 20% the £2.50 beer and no-one bought the cheap beer. This test had the result of reducing income compared to test one – by simply placing a cheaper beer there as an extra option.

In the third test, a third beer was added that was priced at £3.40. In this test, 5% bought the £1.80 beer, 85% bought the £2.50 beer and 10% bought the £3.40 beer. This test showed that adding a more expensive beer rather than a cheaper one resulted in more people buying the £2.50 beer. What these tests showed is that if you are going to offer customers different options, it is better to price higher rather than lower. This will maximise the income you generate and enable you to deliver more social good. It also supports the idea of having a good, better and best option of any products or services you offer.

Different Pricing methods

You can use a number of different pricing methods, as long as you are generating enough sales and surpluses to make your social enterprise sustainable. You want to be remembered as the social enterprise that has traded for 10 years, not the one that closed after 18 months! Below are some of the pricing models that you may choose to use within your organisation.

Breakeven

The absolute minimum price you ought to ever charge is full cost/breakeven. This is in effect the position organisations that have grant funding are in – they receive money to cover the project costs but never make any surpluses on the grants. This is why trading is often better – as you have the freedom to set your own price and make sure you are covering all your costs not just project activity.

Breaking even isn't a great position to be in – you really want surpluses so you can do more social good, develop new innovative products and services, and be entrepreneurial.

Going rate

The next pricing method is going rate – typically used when your product or service is broadly similar to that of your competitors – petrol stations are a great example of this – when one increases their price they all follow! Take care if you decide to use this pricing method, as you are not making your product or service distinctive. If you can describe the value you provide in comparison to your competitors sufficiently well, then you don't need to charge the going rate. If you are predominantly working for the public sector, there is unlikely to be much leeway in terms of pricing and you will have to accept the going rate, unless you provide substantially better quality or outcomes than your competitors and can negotiate a higher price.

Price skimming

This is ideal for products with short life cycles such as apps, computers, mobile phones etc where you have a high price but sell low volumes initially. These products appeal to the person who always has the latest gadget or phone, and are prepared to pay a high price, rather than wait a couple of months until the price is lower.

Prestige pricing

The next method is prestige pricing, where customers are prepared to pay more for higher quality goods and services. If you were offered a genuine Rolex watch for £20 you would wonder what's wrong with it. Our perception is that high price equals high quality, and charging £20 for an exclusive brand would actually damage future sales.

Value Led Pricing

As the example with the beer showed earlier in this chapter, it is important to identify the value you provide and position that appropriately with your other products or services.

Value led pricing is largely defined by the perceived benefits and qualities of your product/service to the customer. This requires you to be able to describe them effectively. If you are unsure ask your customers what difference the product or service has made to their life and how it made them feel.

Price Discrimination

For those of you that provide products or services to a range of different customers a great method is price discrimination – where you charge different types of customers different prices for the same service. Examples include trains (peak, off peak and super off peak, concessions for students and the elderly), concert tickets and restaurants that have special offers for eating early. Social enterprises often do this by offering other social enterprises and charities reduced rates, public sector agencies another slightly higher rate and then commercial organisations a higher rate.

Dynamic Pricing

Dynamic pricing is gaining more popularity particularly as e-commerce has grown. Dynamic pricing is simply about changing your prices in response to supply and demand minute by minute. This isn't the same as price discrimination, as you can price dynamically without knowing anything about your customer's characteristics. But you have to be careful not to be seen as being unfair – for example, if you are providing food at an event and all the other caterers have run out of food, you might increase your prices – but if you increased your prices 4 or 5 times your normal prices, customers would not be impressed and probably refuse to buy from you.

Pricing tips

- Prices should be based on the value to your customer and not on the cost you incur to deliver that product/service
- Increasing your price by a small amount can have a substantial impact on your surpluses
- Products/services can be differentiated from your competitors whatever you sell so you don't have to price match your competitors
- Focus on generating surpluses rather than gaining market share
- Managing price involves making sure that customers understand the value you provide,

and that you have effective processes and quality in place. Managing price is not just about changing prices

Weird things about pricing

Sometimes the purchasing behaviours of customers are weird. If you supply products or services to the public sector you are unlikely to encounter these issues:

- Pricing two similar items at the same price leads to less purchases than if they are priced differently.
- If you want to sell an on-going service talk about the £100 monthly subscription rather than £1,200 annual subscription, as it will appear smaller and more comfortable to the customer.
- Ending prices with a number 9 – for some reason these outsell other prices.
- Making the number bigger reduces sales – by putting the price as £1,000 or £1000.00 instead of £1000 sales reduce.
- Psychological pricing – such as £9.99 instead of £10.00 generates more sales because it is perceived as a lot cheaper.
- Pricing is actually all about marketing – if you can't explain the qualities, attributes and values of your product or service clearly, then your customers won't value it fully, and

you will struggle to achieve the sales price you desire.

Researching and Testing your Pricing

If you are not sure what price to charge, then do some research. Phone your competitors, search on the Internet and go to networking events for your sector.

If you still aren't sure, then test your pricing. Try a particular price and see how much demand you get for your product or service. If a lot of people say the price isn't competitive, it is all about the value. Usually this is due to one of three things:

- You aren't selling the benefits of what you offer well enough
- You are out of line with your competitors' prices for the same service and clients (and can't describe the difference in value you offer)
- You are targeting the wrong people (who are not interested in the value you are trying to sell them, but may be interested in other elements of value)

Another key thing to remember is, if people object to your price and say it is too expensive, if you decide to negotiate and reduce your price, this should be done on the basis that you then change the timescale for delivery, or change the quality or the scope of what you are providing. This then maintains the level of value associated with the original price, and if the customers want to pay less then they will receive less.

KEY POINTS

- Identify the value of your product or service to your customers.
- Move from costing to pricing items.
- Be aware of how having similar items affects sales volumes.
- Test and research your prices if you are unsure.

CHAPTER 8: BUDGETING AND MANAGING YOUR FINANCES

Having financial information

The previous chapter discussed various pricing methods for your products and services. The next step is to produce a budget using your planned sales volumes and prices, and also the associated costs of each of your products and services, plus any organisational running costs and overheads.

Most social entrepreneurs avoid preparing budgets and the management of their organisation's finances as much as possible. This simply delays decision making – and can mean expensive mistakes are made because there is no financial information available.

Working out your budget

Lots of people get hung up about creating a budget for their social enterprise. A sense of fear and overwhelm comes across them, as they panic that they might put the wrong number in their budget. The truth is you cannot get your budget wrong. I will repeat that: YOU CANNOT GET YOUR BUDGET WRONG. The reason why, is because a budget is simply a plan, and as you go along you will learn more and have more information, and so you will update your plan. The other thing about a budget is to remember that it is simply taking everything you described you would do in your business plan and turning it in to numbers. The benefit of having a budget is that is provides you with a financial target for your income and an idea of what you expect your costs to be, so you can track your progress against this.

If you have lots of different projects or funders then it is best to create individual budgets for each project, and then develop an overall organisational budget. The same applies if you have a complex mix of products and services – develop each one separately so you know the costs of each different item.

I always ask clients to tell me how much they would spend on a holiday, including flights, accommodation, meals, entertainment, clothes etc. The amazing thing is that every single person can do this. If you can do this, you can create a budget for your social enterprise, because you would go through exactly the same process. Researching on the Internet, phoning up to ask how much things are and comparing prices between different companies.

What costs to include in a budget

Because a lot of people find preparing budgets difficult, here's a list of typical things to include in your organisation's budget:

- Direct costs of producing your products/services (such as ingredients, delivery costs, packaging, sports equipment, arts and crafts materials etc)
- Accountancy fees
- Legal costs
- Data protection fees
- Insurance (contents, public liability, employer's liability and professional indemnity)
- Licences/memberships
- Website costs and maintenance, hosting and domain fees
- Software
- Computer equipment
- Furniture and fixtures
- Maintenance
- Staff salaries
- Consultant/sub-contractor/freelancer fees
- Volunteer costs and expenses
- Employer's National Insurance
- Pension costs
- Staff training
- Stationery, printing and postage
- Travel costs

- Rent/premises costs
- Use of home as office
- Utilities
- Telephone
- Advertising and marketing costs
- Tax on profits
- Interest expense on loans
- Bank charges

The other really important thing to do with your budget is include a surplus, rather than just getting yourself to breakeven (which is when your income is equal to your expenses).

I tend to start with my costs and include as many as I can straightaway – usually these will be fixed costs or overheads that don't change, regardless of the amount of income I have (such as premises costs). For the example below, let's say these fixed costs and overheads total to £20,000. Then I start working on including the income and costs of the different products and services.

For example if you said in your business plan you will provide training to 100 people, with 60 people being trained in Construction, 25 in Design and 15 in Marketing.

For each item you would have the following, based on the price you have decided to charge:

Item	Number of people trained	Price	Total income
Construction	60	£800	£48,000
Design	25	£400	£10,000
Marketing	15	£500	£7,500
Total	**100**	-	**£65,500**

Then I would look at the direct costs associated with each of the different training programmes. For example, for Construction:

Item	Cost
Tutors	£12,000
Fees to construction firms for work experience	£15,000
Stationery, printing and postage	£800
Rent for training rooms	£6,000
Student equipment and clothing	£2,000
Admin and Finance staff	£1,000
Total Direct Costs	**£36,800**

Let's assume we did a similar exercise for Design and Marketing, and the total direct costs were £2,500 and £1,800 respectively.

Now, I can also add in the fixed costs and overheads at this stage. This is done by allocating some of the £20,000 of overheads to each of my three training programmes. For this example I am going to allocate the overheads based on the number of people training in each programme, so I would have the following:

Item	No. of people trained	Calculation	Total overheads
Construction	60	60/100 X £20,000	£12,000
Design	25	25/100 X £20,000	£5,000
Marketing	15	15/100 X £20,000	£3,000
Total	**100**	-	**£20,000**

In your organisation it may make sense to allocate overheads in a similar way to this. Alternatively, if one of your products or services takes up a lot of staff time then you may want to split overheads based on staff time spent on each product or service.

For Construction I have direct costs of £36,800 and overheads of £12,000 giving a total cost of £48,800, so I have a deficit of £800 as there is only £48,000 of income.

Item	Total Income	Total Cost	Surplus or Deficit
Construction	£48,000	£48,800	-£800
Design	£10,000	£7,500	£2,500
Marketing	£7,500	£4,800	£2,700
Total	**£65,500**	**£61,100**	**£4,400**

Now for construction I would need to decide if I will:

- Increase my price to generate a surplus
- Obtain income from one of the other training programmes to subsidise this
- Look at reducing my costs for delivering this training

If you don't prepare a budget you won't be able to have these conversations and make these decisions as you won't know the true cost of your products and services.

Surpluses are good

Most social entrepreneurs are shy about making profits or surpluses, because they think it would be wrong to do this – but the more profit you make the more difference you can make. Start to have a bigger vision than just breaking even and struggling to survive each year. Make profits and include a surplus in the price you sell products or services for. Because so many social entrepreneurs don't like this idea I always say, whatever number you are thinking of, double it and see what happens. You can always reduce your price or be negotiated down from this point, but if you start at your breakeven point you have nowhere to go except in to loss making and trying to generate additional money to make up for this deficit.

Of course, this concept doesn't always work if you are working with statutory agencies who have fixed prices. In these circumstances you have to decide if you can deliver what is required for the price you are being paid, taking in to consideration the additional monitoring and reporting you will be required to do. If not please walk away from the contract rather than entering into a contract that will run your organisation in to the ground, as has happened to a lot of organisations working within the Work Programme over the last few years.

Reserves

It's advisable to try and build up six months' of reserves for your organisation. This simply means having enough money to cover six months' of running costs if anything happens to your organisation's income. In addition to this you may have specific reserves for redundancies, building projects, research and development, and replacement of computers/equipment. Without reserves your organisation is vulnerable to changes in your income and cash-flow, and has nothing to fall back on in an emergency.

Most organisations write out a reserves policy which is a short statement setting out the planned level of reserves you will have, and also the timescale over which you plan to reach that target.

Cash-flow Forecasts

Once you have created a budget it's also a good idea to create a cash-flow forecast, which looks at when you will receive the money and also when you will be spending the money. The difference between this and a budget is that a budget will be based on when you invoice your customers or when your suppliers invoice you, rather than when the money is transferred and in your bank account. So if you give customers 30 days to pay, but have to pay your suppliers when you order, your cash-flow will reflect this, and show if you will have a shortfall in cash. You can then plan for how you will manage this, by getting an overdraft from the bank or by changing your payment terms. The only time a cash-flow forecast matches exactly with a budget is when your organisation is entirely cash based (so your customers pay cash immediately when they order and you pay all your suppliers in cash when you order goods from them).

Cash really is king, because you can be profitable and show surpluses, but if you do not have any cash in the bank to pay your suppliers and staff your organisation will not survive. To maximise the amount of cash you have:

- Get customers to pay in advance or at the time of ordering where possible. If not, ask for deposits and instalments as the work progresses.
- Take advantage of supplier credit terms rather than paying invoices early (unless they offer substantial discounts for early payment).
- Manage your invoicing and chase for outstanding monies due from your customers.
- Look at the payment terms you offer customers and revise them if necessary.

Managing your finances

Once you have created a budget, cash-flow forecast, tested your prices and included a surplus, you then need to monitor your performance against the budget and cash-flow forecast. I recommend doing this either monthly or quarterly depending on the volume of transactions you have. If you are using online bookkeeping software such as Quickbooks or Xero, you can generate these types of reports automatically. Then look at the difference between what has actually happened and what you planned to happen. Key things to consider are:

- If you are selling less than you planned to – work out why that is happening and decide what action you will take to increase income.
- Do you need to focus on selling more of one item and stop selling another?
- Has there been a sudden increase in demand for a particular item – and should you do more marketing of this to get further sales?
- Why are you selling less than you planned?
- If your costs are higher than planned – what can you do to reduce them or did you not include all your costs in your original budget?
- If it ends up being more expensive that you expected to deliver your product or service, do you need to increase your prices?

Without regular financial reports you can't ask these questions or make appropriate decisions about what needs to change in your organisation.

For your cash-flow identify how long it takes customers to pay and how long you take to pay suppliers, so you can decide if you need to make changes to this. You should regularly update the forecast so you can identify any cash shortfalls in advance which would require an overdraft or loan.

Corporation tax and Income tax

Corporation tax is only payable on the profits (surpluses) you make. This applies to all types of companies, unincorporated organisations and co-ops. Co-ops that are involved in mutual trading between its members do not pay corporation tax on any surpluses generated from this. HMRC has specific criteria that need to be met for this to apply.

If you are a charity, CCBS or CIO you are exempt from corporation tax. You may also be exempt from corporation tax if you do not operate to make a profit or are entirely dependent on grants. However, you need to obtain HMRC's agreement to this.

Self employed and partnerships will be subject to income tax.

Corporation Tax on grants

Grants are usually taxable if they are related to the trade and activities you deliver. However, in most cases there will be no tax liability as the grant income will be cancelled out by the grant expenditure, so there would be no profit/surplus left to be taxed. If the grant is spent on equipment, then the equipment is not eligible for capital allowances.

Financial reporting requirements

It is usual to prepare your accounts for one year periods, with the first set being slightly longer as they will be prepared to the end of the month you set up in. For example, if you set up on 08 August 2015, your first set of accounts would be from that date to 31 August 2016.

You then have nine months to submit these to Companies House if you are a company, or seven months to the Financial Conduct Authority if you are a Mutual Society (Co-op/CBS/CCBS). Charity Commission require accounts to be submitted within 10 months. In addition to accounts, tax returns are submitted to HMRC for unincorporated organisations, co-ops, CBSs and companies within 12 months after the end of the accounting period.

For self employed individuals and partnerships the accounts are due 31 January following the end of the tax year along with the tax returns and are submitted to HMRC, i.e. for accounts prepared up to 05 April 2016 these must be submitted by 31 January 2017.

The Regulatory bodies also require annual returns to be completed. Companies House has recently replaced their Annual Return with a Confirmation Statement. There are small fees for submitting these, except Charity Commission who do not currently charge for this.

KEY POINTS

- Spend time preparing a budget so you know what income and costs you will have.
- Make sure you generate surpluses.
- Develop a reserve policy and start to build up reserves.
- Recognise the importance of cash and manage your organisation's cash-flow.
- Monitor your finances regularly.
- Prepare annual accounts and tax returns and submit these on time.

Further information:

Book-keeping software: www.quickbooks.co.uk and www.xero.com/uk

Business plan templates (includes financial templates): www.gov.uk/write-business-plan

Cash-flow template: www.startuploans.co.uk/cash-flow-forecast-template/

Reporting and regulatory requirements:
Charity Commission:
www.gov.uk/government/organisations/charity-commission

Companies House:
www.gov.uk/government/organisations/companies-house

CIC Regulator:
www.gov.uk/government/organisations/office-of-
the-regulator-of-community-interest-companies

CBS & Co-operatives:
www.fca.org.uk/firms/mutual-societies

Co-operatives UK: http://www.uk.coop/

CHAPTER 9: STAFF – EMPLOYING THE RIGHT PEOPLE

Making the transition to having staff

When you first set up your social enterprise having staff is likely to be just a dream. It's probably going to be just you, or you and one other person. This means you will be doing pretty much everything, as already mentioned – sales, marketing, providing the services, producing the products, delivering the activities, IT, website, social media, finance, invoicing, book-keeping, cleaning, and everything else you can think of.

But, from the beginning you need to "Begin with the end in mind" – what is your plan if you are ill or decide to stop running the social enterprise? By thinking about this, as you grow your social enterprise, you can start to move to a situation where you are only doing the things you love and everything else is done by other people. When I had my accountancy business, I knew that I would sell the business one day and as part of that plan I developed a staff team around me that could run the business without my input. Your social enterprise needs to run if you are away for two weeks holiday, without you being phoned and emailed several times a day by staff panicking about things. The way I did this was to include my staff in the things I did, let them lead on things I would previously do – such as a client meeting, and set them objectives for new work activities they needed to complete.

When I became pregnant I knew I had about nine months to develop a Mini Me to run the business whilst I was on maternity leave. By this time, there were only a few things that I exclusively did, so it was not difficult to train the staff in these remaining things. You never know what is going to happen to you, so if you are afraid to share what you know because your staff might run off with your ideas and start a social enterprise to compete with you, then the chances are they will leave because you are not helping to develop them and build their skills. It's better to keep good staff, train and develop them, so they can do what you do only in their own way.

The Recruitment Process

Because I have been involved with a number of large scale businesses and organisations that had very complex recruitment processes, with several stages of interviews and tests, which are often excessive and not necessarily providing any insight into the individual's ability to do the job, I have found the following work well:

- A defined person specification and job description – clearly identifying what you are looking for and the type of personal attributes you desire, as well as stating the main activities and responsibilities of the role.

- An application process that will help you to identify if the person has some or all of these attributes and skills.
- A process for scoring applicants so they can be shortlisted for interview.
- A standard set of questions you use for interviews. Depending on the role you may include some form of test or presentation as part of the interview process.
- A formal contract of employment (a written statement of employment particulars) and induction process.

Person specification and Job Description

I have seen lots of social entrepreneurs create really bad job roles. They try to create a full time job which in reality is several part time jobs doing different functions, and then they call it Administrator or Office Manager. What they really need is someone to do marketing, someone to do the book-keeping/credit control and someone to do some administration.

Be specific about what you require, otherwise you will end up with something completely different. If you aren't sure what you require then take someone on as self employed for a few hours a week for a short time period, and then when you have evolved this role in to what you need you can then employ someone. The Job Description will include the main purpose of the role, the main duties and responsibilities, who the person reports to, if they manage any staff, and any reporting requirements.

The person specification should identify characteristics, experience, qualifications and personal traits you would like, and identify them as either essential for the role or desirable.

Application process

For the application process I recommend asking specific questions or having an application form, rather than accepting CVs, because CVs are often very generic and not specific to the role you are advertising. This will make it more difficult to assess the applicant's suitability for the role.

If you ask people to fill in an application form, and make it clear that you are not accepting CVs, if they attach their CV and in response to the questions on the form write "see attached CV", I would not score or shortlist them for the role. If they are not able to follow simple instructions regarding the application process or to take the time to answer the questions, I think it says a lot about their enthusiasm for the role.

Avoiding recruitment issues

Although the extra effort of creating a person specification and application form may be time consuming upfront, it is worthwhile as it will save you time and potential issues in the future. About 12 years ago I was involved in recruiting for an IT tutor, to teach adults IT skills, and nearly 30 applications were received. One of the applicants was an electrical engineer who had no IT experience or teaching experience, and when he was scored against the criteria for the role his total was 3 points out of a possible 25.

We proceeded with notifying the highest scoring applicants that we wished to interview them, but interestingly, a couple of days after the application deadline the electrical engineer phoned to ask when his interview was! I remember finding the phone conversation very odd, but I was able to look at his score against the criteria and simply state that unfortunately he had not been shortlisted for interview as other applicants had been scored more highly than him.

He then emailed asking for feedback on why he hadn't been shortlisted and what the process was for shortlisting applicants. But because everything was documented and each applicant was scored independently by two people, it was very easy to respond to this query.

What this taught me was no matter how irrelevant the applicant's skills, experience and responses to the questions may be, you must still follow a specific process when shortlisting and interviewing, so you cannot be accused of being unfair or biased.

Shortlisting process

When you review the applications you have received you need to have a standard process for shortlisting people for interview. This could include having a checklist (that includes the essential and desirable items from your person specification) that you score applications against. This makes the process of reducing lots of applicants to a small number for interview much easier and objective as well. Generally, I score the applicants and also get someone else to independently score them, and then we share our scores. If there are differences we agree the final score jointly.

At this point I aim to reduce the number of individuals I am interviewing down to a maximum of four, ideally just three. The reason being that interviewing more than three or four individuals usually leaves you unsure who to offer the job to. By being strict and only interviewing the top three you are making your decision much easier.

The Interview

For the interview process, I have specific questions that I ask all applicants, and then depending on the information they have submitted I may ask for clarification about something on their application.

Having employed people just on the basis of an interview and their explanation of what they know, I have found some form of test to be highly effective at showing whether the person can actually do what they claim to be able to do. The only exceptions I make to this are when I am recruiting for a role where no experience is required, but I may still ask them to type a letter or something similar to show they can use a computer and spell (or spell check) a document! When I first wanted to recruit an Accounts Manager I interviewed three people, and each of them stated they had lots of experience in accounts, having done degrees or accountancy qualifications. However, when they were asked to look at some figures on a spreadsheet and correct the errors, none of them could do it. I didn't appoint any of them to the role and re-advertised it instead.

It may seem as if these processes are overly complex, but you are looking for an individual who you can work with, who is capable of doing what you require and who you will be paying for this work. If they aren't able to do their job role as a result of you rushing the recruitment process because you just employed the first person who applied, then you will wish you had invested more time at the beginning, rather than having to spend a lot of time on performance managing the individual, dismissing them and beginning the recruitment process again.

Interestingly, what I have found with many social enterprises, where they have employed someone who isn't able to do the job they keep them. And rather than resolving the issue they hire other people to do the things this person can't do or do it themselves. One of my biggest horror stories is with a charity that had been in existence for over 150 years, and it felt like most of the staff had been there that long. The organisation was the most inefficient I have ever seen, but it had never made anyone redundant. When funding for a job role ended they either created a new role for the person to move in to or kept them on in their current role without having any funding for that post. Eventually it became unsustainable, and they had nearly 60 people whose roles were not funded – and were basically using up the reserves. In the end the charity had to close. Whilst employing disadvantaged individuals may be part of your social purpose, this has to be balanced alongside being financially sustainable and viable; and providing a quality service to customers.

Written statement of employment particulars

Once you have selected the individual you wish to employ you need to send them a written statement of employment particulars, setting out the terms and conditions of their employment. I typically have a three month probationary period, and only after this time do I make their role permanent. I have found three months is sufficient to know if someone is going to be able to do the job and their motivation and enthusiasm, as well as their ability to work with others and deal with customers.

Induction

It is beneficial to provide new employees with an induction, which takes them through the key organisational policies, procedures and ways of doing things. It is also an opportunity to complete any mandatory training – such as safeguarding, equal opportunities and diversity etc.

Training and development

You can never provide too much training and development to your staff. There's a great quote about What if we train them and they leave? And the response is What if we don't and they stay? This is so true. I have never minded investing in training for staff, because it shows you care about their progression, want to give them opportunities to develop new skills and to broaden their role. Sometimes it will backfire and they will leave shortly after being trained. Of course, you get a bit stressed and sad, but when I decided to train young people to be accountants I didn't expect them to stay working for me forever. I expected the job to provide a stepping stone to their next role, and although that meant staff probably only staying in the role for four years maximum, I was happy to do this because it was part of my social purpose.

Appraisals

It is a good idea to have annual appraisals, and also to set objectives for performance. Many organisations have weekly supervision sessions, where workload and completion of tasks are checked. This should link in to your appraisal system – where you review performance at regular intervals. If you have a probationary period when you take on a new employee, towards the end of the probationary period you would complete an appraisal to identify if their probationary period needs extending or if you will end the probationary period. In the first year I like to complete appraisals at 3, 6 and 12 months, then annually thereafter.

Performance management and dismissal

This is an area most social enterprises shy away from, because they believe that employing people is good, and it would be bad to sack someone. I have been to visit so many Chief Executives who are unfortunate enough to have staff that are no good at their jobs, and when I ask what they did when the person first started, they will reply nothing. If you don't performance manage a person as soon as you notice they are not doing their job properly it is almost impossible to do this later, because you have accepted that standard of work.

Maintaining your social purpose through your recruitment

Whenever I recruit for staff I always ask them what they know about social enterprise, ask about their values and discuss my organisation's values with them as well. I also ask them what difference they think it will make working for a social enterprise. To me skills can usually be taught but values are something the person must have to start with.

It's a great idea to spend some time when you first set up, thinking about what your organisation's ethos and values will be. These will be important as you grow and expand, and provide any staff, Board members and customers with information about how you operate.

Typical values might include:

- Accessible to all

- Professional
- Honest
- Dedicated
- Innovative
- Passionate
- Caring

KEY POINTS

- Have a clear job description for each role whether that's for a paid or voluntary position.
- Set objectives and manage your staff.
- Have clear processes for dealing with performance issues.
- Invest in your staff and their training and personal development.

Further information:

Written statement of employment particulars guidance and template:

http://www.acas.org.uk/index.aspx?articleid=1577

www.gov.uk/employment-contracts-and-conditions/written-statement-of-employment-particulars

CHAPTER 10: EMPLOYMENT ISSUES

Employed versus self employed

When you require additional help you have a choice between employing someone or paying them as self employed. Providing the individual is not in reality an employee you can look at paying them as a self employed individual. HMRC have a set of rules they use to decide if someone is employed or self employed, which includes the following:

- The right to provide a substitute – if you are employed you cannot send a replacement, whereas if you are self employed you can send someone else to complete the work.
- Mutual obligation – as an employee you are obliged to do as your employer requests and your employer is obliged to provide you work, whereas if you are self employed you can turn down the work if you wish and they are under no obligation to offer you any work.
- Control – an employer will control where, what, when and how the work is done, whereas if you are self employed you will have control over the majority of these.
- Provision of equipment – an employee will usually have the equipment required to do the work supplied by the employer, whereas

if you are self employed you will normally supply the equipment yourself.

- Financial risk/profit – as an employee you will normally have little financial risk as you will be paid (unless you are commission based) and you won't benefit from any profits generated (unless you are part of a bonus scheme linked to profits). If you are self employed you bear the risk if the work takes longer than anticipated and will be liable to correct anything at your own expense – but you also potentially make a profit if the work is completed more quickly.
- Contract length – as an employee the contract is usually open ended with no fixed end date. Whereas, if you are self employed you will usually be working for a fixed term contract.

Other things to consider to identify if you can be classed as self employed relate to the viability and independence of your self employment business:

- Do you have employees?
- Do you have a website and marketing materials?
- Do you have other clients in addition to your own organisation?

If you were previously employed by the organisation, and then switch to self employed, but continue to carry out the same role HMRC would challenge that you are genuinely self employed.

The main difference for your social enterprise is that usually self employed individuals will be cheaper as you do not have to pay Employer's National Insurance Contributions and pension contributions on top of the individual's salary. But with the Employer's National Insurance Allowance meaning you do not pay the first £3,000 of contributions, it may not make much financial difference.

There is also the Intermediaries Legislation (IR35) which treats the individual as an employee. This applies where the individual has their own company and invoices the organisation for their work, but if it was not for the limited company they would be treated as an employee of the organisation. In these circumstances, any income received by the individual through their own limited company must be paid out as salary and subject to PAYE.

If you decide to take someone on as self employed please issue them with a contract detailing what they are expected to deliver, the timescales and the payment terms as a minimum.

Directors – self employed or salaried

This is one of the most popular questions that social entrepreneurs ask, as they are keen to receive their income from the organisation in a way that is least costly to the organisation and themselves.

However, there are specific rules that mean if you are a Director of your organisation you are treated as an office holder by HMRC, and this means any payments you receive for your role as a Director must be as salary and subject to PAYE. There is the option to treat any activities that do not form part of your Director role as self employed, providing there is sufficient distinction between the two roles. So, if you are able to split your strategic and legal responsibilities as a Director from delivery on programmes/projects it may be possible to do this. It is also better if you also have other work you do as a self employed individual in addition to the work you invoice your organisation for, otherwise it would look like an artificial separation of your income simply to avoid paying tax. If you are working full time for your organisation then this route is not generally recommended.

There are also different rules in place if your organisation is a charity – as there are restrictions on the number of Directors (trustees) that can be paid, and they cannot be paid for the duties as a trustee – only for additional support and services they provide.

Developing a mini you

This is all about shifting from working in to working on your business. Having a mini you, doesn't mean having someone identical to you, but it does mean having an individual or several individuals who can do various bits of your role in your absence, so the organisation is not dependent on you to continue in existence.

Partly through my own approach to running my organisation and as a consequence of having a long term piece of consultancy work that meant I was out of the office three days a week for over 18 months, I was lucky to build a team around me who could do almost everything I did. When I became pregnant, I made a commitment to take maternity leave, and so during 2014, I trained the staff in the other bits of my role.

It may sound as if I am doing myself out of a job, but I completely believe that everyone is replaceable in an organisation and that the strongest organisations are those that are not dependent on one person.

By 2015 I was no longer needed in my social enterprise operationally. The fantastic thing that happened was I had time to create new services, to focus on business growth and even though I was only working two days a week the organisation's income grew substantially.

As far as anyone buying is concerned you are the organisation and the organisation is you. Then as your organisation grows you take on additional staff to help. But this has little impact on your working day. Everyone still wants you, and although your staff may be competent no-one is considered as good as you.

My tips for making this transition to where customers will build relationships and work with other staff members are:

- Get the right team around you – what skills and character traits do others need to replace your skill set?
- Invest in your staff – make sure they access all the training and development they need to do their jobs and set them clear objectives for their personal development.
- Get input from your staff – build a culture where they can say what they think and their input is incorporated in to how you grow and run your organisation.
- Enable staff to make decisions – give your staff the authority to do things without you being there. This means you have to trust

others to do what you would do (and don't be worried if they do it in a different way to you), and give them the reassurance that if they are not sure they can ask you.

- Once they have mastered number 4, make yourself unavailable – if you are always available your staff will always ask you what to do. By making yourself unavailable for a few hours they have to take the giant step of making a decision in your absence when a customer is waiting for an answer.
- Treat mistakes as learning opportunities – there will inevitably be some mistakes as you let go of things, but in most cases these are manageable mistakes and your staff will definitely remember the right thing to do next time.
- Provide rewards – incentivise staff through good working conditions, pay and other rewards. This doesn't have to be big rewards and could be as simple as taking them out for a meal.
- Have regular reviews – discuss the plans with staff, review these regularly, identify potential issues and then work out how you will overcome these.
- Focus on the end result - keep the big picture in mind at all times – you want an organisation that you work on not one you have to work in every day.

Volunteers

To me volunteers are no different to employees – and you should treat the process of recruiting, managing and training volunteers the same. This means having real roles rather than letting people help out for a few hours. Often volunteers are coming from backgrounds of disadvantage and have been out of the labour market for a long time period, so they require additional support. The only area I am cautious about with volunteers is when they are expected to do exactly the same as a paid employee – because I would expect you to pay them. JobcentrePlus and large supermarkets have been criticised for offering unpaid work experience to individuals, when in reality they would normally pay people to carry out those roles. Many organisations have extensive volunteer programmes, but these are usually managed and co-ordinated so the person benefits from the volunteering experience, whereas small organisations often don't have the resources to support volunteers. To me there is a balance to be had between having volunteers, managing them and the financial implications of employing someone instead of having volunteers.

The same applies to your Board members – have a proper recruitment process and identify skills gaps in your Board. I have recently joined the Board of Start Again Project CIC because they identified they needed someone with a financial background and also with experience in social impact measurement and reporting.

Organisational Policies

When you take on staff you will require a range of policies to be in place around:

- Disciplinary
- Grievance
- Holiday and Sickness
- Training and Development

It's worthwhile creating some form of staff handbook which incorporates all these things. As well as documents and policies for staff, you will also need policies for common areas such as:

- Health and Safety
- Financial Management
- Environmental
- Equal Opportunities/Diversity
- Safeguarding
- Risk Assessment

KEY POINTS

- Check the status of an individual to see whether they are actually self employed or if the reality of the situation is that they are an employee.

- Be aware of how Directors must be paid.
- Develop staff to take on your role and responsibilities.
- Have policies and procedures in place to support how you run your organisation.

Further information:

Employed versus self employed guidance: www.gov.uk/hmrc

The best site for numerous templates including Contract for services template for self employed individuals, Employment contract templates, Staff Handbook template and HR Policy manual templates is:

http://www.human-resource-solutions.co.uk

CHAPTER 11: MARKETING YOUR WAY TO SUCCESS

Marketing is all about you

Many people really struggle when it comes to marketing their social enterprise. I have found that the best way to market your organisation is not by spending lots of money. There are several simple and very effective ways you can market your organisation. The most important of these is to talk to people about your organisation wherever you go – you never know who you might meet. Just by sharing what you do you can benefit enormously because even if that person isn't interested they probably know someone who will be. If you can talk positively and easily about the benefits your organisation provides, you will become the best marketing tool for your organisation.

Another thing to consider is being able to explain your passion and your Why (Why you set up the organisation) in around one minute. This is sometimes referred to as an elevator pitch, where you only have until the elevator doors open to get someone interested. Being able to do this is often the thing that makes the difference when trying to secure funding, investment or new customers. Your passion for your organisation will engage others and make them want to know more.

Describe your ideal customer and their problem

Nowadays everyone talks about your ideal customer and understanding their issue. If you can get to grips with this, you can then identify the perfect product or service to solve their issue. Your product or service should either move someone further away from the issue or closer to happiness.

The customer for many social enterprises will be a mix of the general public and other people such as commissioners and funders. See Chapter 6 which discusses how to identify your customers and Chapter 7 which discusses the perceived value to customers.

Building a brand

One important thing to do is to develop a brand – which will identify and distinguish you from your competitors. This includes having standard colour schemes in your marketing materials, the style and way you talk and communicate in your marketing, what your organisation stands for and include a logo. These things won't market your organisation on their own, but they will be a way for people to identify your organisation.

With marketing your services, the key thing is to test out different methods until you find the ones that work for your organisation. People will only buy from people they know, like and trust. It typically takes a minimum of three pieces of marketing before a person will consider buying from your organisation. The average is around seven pieces. This can be reduced where people have been recommended or referred, as they will usually ask people they trust, and if you are recommended that relationship of trust exists immediately.

Using social media and websites

Social media nowadays is one of the key ways to market your organisation. I personally have found LinkedIn to be the most useful site for promoting the work I do, but I know many people who have great success with Facebook and also through creating their own Facebook Groups. Organisations that have products have also used Instagram very effectively to showcase their work.

My advice with social media is don't try to be everywhere. Pick three places where your target clients hang out and use them – whether that's Snapchat, Instagram, Facebook, Twitter, LinkedIn, YouTube or one of the plethora of other social media sites. Try to automate the process of posting information as much as possible using Hootsuite or Bufferapp for example.

The optimum number of posts on each site is three per day. If you can't think of anything to say, look

at some of the content curator or newsfeed sites –
so you can simply share content they have found.
Back your social media presence up with a website
that will confirm you exist. Your website does not
need to be complex, but it needs to include:

- What you do
- Who you work with
- Some background information about your
  organisation and the staff/Board members
- How to contact you
- A blog or news feature that is regularly
  updated
- E-commerce/shopping cart if you have
  products or services that can be purchased
  online

Case study: RnR Organisation

RnR Organisation was founded by Pauline Roche
and Ted Ryan, and is an example of a social
enterprise that has used social media and
networking to build its client base. Here Pauline
explains more:

We wanted to run our own social enterprise to work
with community groups and charities with incomes
from £0 to £500,000 to improve their businesses.
We also wanted to assert ourselves as VCSE
thought leaders, write about smart cities and how
the voluntary sector should be involved, including
raising organisations awareness of the importance

of access to data/data sharing (including open data) by organising #techforgood and #data4good meetups, events and groups such as Net Squared Midlands, VCSSCamp (unconference for voluntary sector infrastructure organisations), Open Data Camp (unconference for people interested in open data), and open data groups (West Midlands Open Data Forum, Birmingham Open Data Institute and Open Mercia).

The main way people hear about our work is through colleagues in membership networks we are involved with who talk about us, including colleagues in the co-working space where we are members (Impact Hub Birmingham in Digbeth), Digbeth Social Enterprise Quarter, BSSEC and SEWM.

We also get referrals from satisfied clients who recommend us to people and organisations in their networks. We are active on popular social media channels - LinkedIn, Twitter and Facebook

The advice we give to other organisations is build up your networks, both physical and virtual (especially LinkedIn and Twitter). On LinkedIn make connections with people you know, join relevant groups and learn from how others in your field describe themselves and their business to make yourself more noticeable.

On Twitter have a personal and a business account, identify popular hashtags and follow/contribute to those conversations but don't feel you have to be in every conversation. Follow the most interesting people, wherever they are in the world. Volunteer on a regular basis in an organisation you like in order to share and hone your skills and to meet like-minded people; and seek opportunities to give back and support others.

The biggest issue for us has been the lack of infrastructure that understands the need for digital skills and time to do everything we want to. Also, many of the groups who want to work with us are not able to buy in our support due to a lack of funding and we sometimes work with them to raise those funds.

In 10 years' time we see RnR Organisation at the forefront of digital and data literacy development in the UK charitable and voluntary sector, especially amongst smaller organisations and those working with marginalised groups.

RnR Organisation is a #techforgood social enterprise that provides support to smaller voluntary, community and social enterprise organisations (VCSE) to use technology to demonstrate their impact as they engage with changes in the public funding environment. We work with three social change-making communities:

- Our Community of Interest: Social Businesses that affect people's lives and make a difference.
- Our Community of Geography: where we live in Balsall Heath and Sparkbrook.
- Our Community of Culture: Minority Cultural activity - we are part of the Irish Diaspora, immigrants to England and allies to other minority arts and cultural activities.

RnR.Organisation@gmail.com

www.RnROrganisation.co.uk

@RnRWorks

@paulineroche

Webinars and online videos

When you search for anything on the Internet, the top ranked search items are usually videos. This is because video is given preference in search engines over other types of content, so if you can, try to incorporate videos in your websites, blog posts or on social media. On Facebook, Facebook Live is given priority in feeds to other types of content and also priority over videos that link to YouTube or other external sites.

Webinars are another great way to showcase what you know, and these can be delivered live, pre-recorded or recorded whilst you are delivering it live. I have run free webinar programmes on social impact measurement, and found they are a useful way to demonstrate your knowledge and expertise in a particular field.

Networking and events

Going to events and networking is one of the best ways to market your organisation, particularly when you are first starting out and may not know anyone in your sector or other social enterprises. The best networking events for me have been those specifically for social enterprises, because they have led to partnerships and joint working, and the people I met shared similar values and ethos to me. However, if you are interested in developing partnerships with businesses or obtaining corporate sponsors, or securing contracts with the public sector then you will need to identify the appropriate networks to attend.

With events, you can run your own, speak at other peoples' events or simply attend the event - as long as you are willing to speak to people and network you will find these events useful. When you first start there is a tendency to think you need to go to every event out there. But you will find that it is very often the same people at every event, and this doesn't make it worthwhile to keep going to so many events. Be selective, and go to events that are really relevant to what you do.

Buy Social ethos

There are several organisations that provide endorsement for you as a social enterprise, and this can lead to additional marketing of your social enterprise. This includes the Social Enterprise Mark accreditation, SEUK's version of this and also the Fairtrade movement as well. If you are trying to raise awareness of the fact you are a social enterprise with your customers then this is something worth considering.

Referrals and recommendations

When I was running my accountancy CIC I relied on referrals and recommendations for the majority of my new clients. To get to this point took four years, but it was worth the time and effort that was spent building good client relationships. You may want to consider offering some form of reward for referrals – either as a discount off future purchases, vouchers or cash, or some other incentive.

Offer something free

So many people do this now it is almost expected that if you want to engage with a customer you will offer them something free. This could range from free consultations, e-books, guides, templates, samples etc.

Paper based marketing

About three years ago I stopped producing leaflets and printed marketing materials because no-one ever asked for them. The majority of enquiries were via the website or email and the information was sent as a pdf document. Those that I met face to face just asked for my business card rather than a leaflet. However, leaflets can be very useful if you are targeting a geographical area rather than people with specific characteristics. Also, sending items in the post is now a novel way to get a potential customer's attention, as people tend to receive less items in the post.

KEY POINTS

- You are the best marketing tool for your organisation because of your passion.
- Have a website and use social media, but be selective about which social media you use.
- Build relationships with people to develop referrals and recommendations.

- Don't attend every event or network – pick the ones that are relevant.
- Test out different marketing methods and see which ones work for your organisation.

Further information:

Logo design: www.logomaker.com

Website design: www.firststopwedesign.co.uk

Automating social media: www.hootsuite.com and www.bufferapp.com

Content curation and newsfeed: www.feedly.com and www.scoop.it

Webinars: www.zoom.us

Buy Social: www.socialenterprisemark.org.uk; www.socialenterpriseuk.org.uk; www.buysocialdirectory.org.uk and www.fairtrade.org.uk

SECTION THREE

CHAPTER 12: FINANCING YOUR SOCIAL ENTERPRISE

When it comes to setting up your social enterprise or growing it, there are a number of options available to obtain finance.

Own investment

Setting up a social enterprise will inevitably cost you money. Even if you secure a start-up loan or grant, you will still have invested time and some money to get to that point. Unless you secure a contract or grant straight away you may also be volunteering your time to start with. There is a fine balance to be had because I have known people who are so passionate about their social enterprise that they have put themselves and their family in to serious debt and hardship whilst trying to develop their social enterprise. I believe it is important to show your commitment and dedication to your social enterprise, but without putting your home or family at risk.

Selling products or services

Trading is what social enterprises are about – and it's the ultimate sustainability providing you have the mix of products and customers (as described in Chapter 6). By having products and services that you make a surplus on you are able to finance things like the following:

- Training and development of staff
- Recruitment of staff
- Piloting and testing of new services
- Research and development
- Innovation
- Capital equipment
- Redundancies
- Unforeseen expenses
- Investment in other assets/businesses

The other great thing about generating your own surpluses and cash reserves is that no-one can tell you how to spend them as they were internally generated.

Grants/Donations

Often you will be able to get grants to start up your social enterprise. A lot of grant makers like new organisations as they consider them to be innovate, working with a priority client group or operating in a geographical area where there are many other organisations.

Alternatively, you can hold fundraising events or ask for donations. If you hold local community events, you may raise around £500-600 after you have paid out for the various expenses of organising and running the event. However, if you

134

can get corporates and businesses involved in your fundraising it will be much easier to raise larger sums of money.

Businesses are keen to sponsor events and organisations providing its beneficial to them. To make it beneficial you ideally must offer at least one of the following:

- Marketing of their product/service
- Involvement of their staff
- Volunteering opportunities for their staff
- Local to their premises

Crowdfunding

For the publication of this book I tested crowdfunding. Partly so I could share my experience in this book and partly because it was such a simple process to set up a project and make it public. What I learnt was you need to mobilise people quickly and get them to take action. My first attempt to crowdfund didn't hit its target – it was just over £200 short, and I had tried to do it in 10 days. I decided to try again and do it over 8 days. I exceeded the target the second time around. The reason for this was that people needed time to see I was crowdfunding – which the first attempt provided, and then time to take action. But the recommended maximum time for a crowdfunding campaign is 30 days, and ideally not more than 21 days. So if you are planning to do this, get people prepared. Start sharing and promoting what you are doing in advance, so you have a crowd to notify once your campaign goes live. The other interesting thing about crowdfunding is that it is rarely people you don't know who back you. It is typically friends, family and other connections – and this is usually about 90% of your backers and around 10% are people that just like the look of your project.

The key things to remember with crowdfunding are to offer people something in exchange for them backing your project that they will want. With my crowdfunding it is effectively a donation as the money is not repayable. However, there are some sites where you can crowdfund loans or share investments. In this scenario the lenders expect their money to be repaid, possibly with interest as well, and the share investors expect to receive dividends and a repayment of their share investment at some point in the future.

Shares/Loans

There are a whole range of different types of share and loan investments available to organisations depending on their legal structure. The key thing about investment is that organisations with loans or external shareholders perform better than those without, because they have to pay interest or dividends to these individuals. Detailed in the next section are a number of share (equity) and loan (debt) options, and their availability based on your legal structure.

What's available with your legal structure?

Charities can only take on loans as they are set up as limited by guarantee companies or unincorporated organisations with no shares. Most social enterprises and Community Interest Companies (CICs) are also set up as companies limited by guarantee so can also only have loans. Approximately 10% of CICs are limited by share, so they can issue different types of shares. There are increasing numbers of CICs registering with this type of legal structure, but this still limits the number of social enterprises that can issue shares. Community Benefit Societies and Co-operatives can issue loans or community shares which are withdrawable.

Loans (Debt)

Nearly all social enterprises and charities can take on loans (debt) unless they have restrictions in their Articles or governing documents. Loans can be:

Fixed interest, variable interest, performance related, secured or unsecured, and have early repayment charges, the option to defer or take a payment holiday, and mixed financial and social return requirements.

Pros

- Ideal if you receive payments in arrears for delivery of services
- Helps with cash flow issues
- Good for capital purchases as payments are secured against the asset
- Have been shown to enable quicker growth as organisations must become more commercial in order to meet the loan repayments
- The lender doesn't receive a share of the organisation's surplus/profits (unless loan interest is performance related and linked to profits), so any growth and surpluses benefit the organisation rather than the lender.
- Profit linked loans/performance related loans for CICs have their interest rate capped at 20% so the organisation knows the maximum amount of interest that will be paid. This cap does not affect other types of loans.
- The lender has no control over your business and once the loan is repaid the relationship ends.
- Unless interest paid is variable or performance related then it is possible to

forecast accurately the interest payments and these can be planned for in advance.

- Interest is an allowable expense for tax purposes, which reduces the cost of borrowing for social enterprises that pay corporation tax.

Cons

- The loan capital has to be repaid at some point unlike equity which, unless redeemable (or withdrawable for Co-ops and Community Benefit Societies), is unlikely to be repaid.
- Cashflow is required for both interest and the capital repayments which can cause difficulties if the business does not grow as planned.
- There may be restrictions on the organisation that stop it from taking on further loans or starting new areas of delivery/trading.
- Although less common nowadays, Directors may be required to provide personal guarantees for the loan capital.
- Most investors will still expect a commercial rate of interest regardless of the organisation's social return and social impact, so doing good things for society does not reduce the cost of having a loan.
- There may be charges for defaults, late payments, early repayment plus

administration or set up charges that will add to the cost of the loan.

Equity

Equity (shares) investments are only available to a small number of social enterprises that are companies limited by share, or a CBS or Co-op.

Pros

- The investor takes all the risk. If the organisation is not successful you are not personally liable and do not have to pay the investor back. The investor won't receive a dividend if the company doesn't make any profits, and if the company makes larger profits the dividends paid can be larger.
- Most shareholders take a long term view and do not expect to have their share capital repaid in the short term.
- The shares can increase in value based on the value of the organisation, so the investor could sell the shares for more than they were purchased for.
- Social finance organisations will often want to participate in the organisation actively, by attending Board meetings or providing an additional Director for the Board.

Cons

- You are giving away a share of the organisation and if the shares are ordinary shares the investor will be able to vote and have a say in business decisions. This is why most people restrict the amount of shareholding they are prepared to give away so they don't lose control of the organisation.
- Alternatively, you can set up different classes of shares. This is something many of our clients have done so they don't give away any of the control or voting rights in the organisation. A second class of shares can have different restrictions on them to the ordinary shares, and you can set the dividend amounts so they are fixed in a similar way to interest payments on loans, or alternatively vary them based on the amount of profit you make.
- The main issue is that the organisation must make a profit in order to pay the dividends so if the organisation does not perform as well as expected the investors will receive no return.
- The maximum dividends that can be paid for CICs is 35% of the organisation's profits, so investors may only receive a small return.

- Shareholders are the last to be paid, after all the other expenses and any loan interest have been paid.
- Dividends are not tax deductible, so organisations that pay corporation tax will pay tax of 20% of the amount of dividends paid out.

Redeemable shares

Redeemable shares are shares that have a set date for the organisation to buy the shares back from the investor, usually at the same value as was initially invested. This is beneficial where the original owners do not want to give control of the company away in the long term. It is also good where the organisation expects to generate large surpluses and be able to buy back the shares in a short time period, or to provide investors with the flexibility to ask for their investment back at certain times. Any class of shares can be redeemable.

Quasi equity

Quasi equity is financing that reflects some of the characteristics of shares (equity) but not all. Two examples of this are convertible loans and revenue participation loans.

Convertible Loans

Convertible loans are loans that can be converted to equity (shares) at some point in the future. This gives the organisation certainty over the interest payments initially (typically for 3-5 years) and then the investor has the option to convert their loan to a shareholding or have the loan repaid. This benefits the investor as they can benefit from larger dividend payments in comparison to the level of interest they were receiving, providing the organisation has grown sufficiently to make the dividend payments larger. With CICs because of the dividend cap unless the organisation makes a lot of profit, being able to distribute 35% of profit as dividends may still only provide a small return to the investor. This option is not available to Limited by Guarantee companies or charities.

Revenue Participation Loans

Revenue participation loans are where the interest rate is linked to the increase in turnover the organisation achieves. This is ideal if there are uncertainties or variations regarding what the turnover will be, as the organisation will pay a lower return if turnover does not increase much, and a higher return if turnover increases more. This provides the investor with more risk, as they benefit if the organisation does well, but will also receive less if the organisation performs badly.

From the organisation's perspective, increasing turnover does not necessarily mean there will be an increase in profit/surpluses so this could be a costly type of investment if profit does not increase in line with the increase in turnover. Variations on this type of financing include where the investment is linked to an increase in turnover for specific activities eg for trading income but not grant income, or for increases over a certain threshold.

The benefits of quasi equity are that where the investment is more like debt there is no dilution of ownership and control for social enterprises, and securing the investment will often be less time consuming and costly than trying to obtain equity investments.

KEY POINTS

- Grants and funding are usually available to help start up an organisation, or to test innovate ideas, but funders like to support organisations that show they can become sustainable and not continue to be dependent on grants.
- Crowdfunding is a great way to engage your community in raising money for your organisation.
- Investment is becoming more common place amongst social enterprises, through loans,

144

shares and quasi equity, as the availability of funding reduces.

Further information:

Start up grants, support and also grants for growing/scaling up organisations: www.unltd.org.uk and www.the-sse.org

Start up loans: www.startuploans.co.uk

Other loans: www.charitybank.org; www.triodos.co.uk; www.unity.co.uk; www.cafonline.org and www.responsiblefinance.org.uk

Crowdfunding and peer to peer lending: www.kickstarter.com; www.communitychest.co.uk; www.justgiving.com/crowdfunding and www.crowdcube.com

Grants and funding: www.fundingcentral.org.uk; www.biglotteryfund.org.uk; andwww.governmentfunding.org.uk

Grants to become investment and contract ready: www.bigpotential.org.uk

CHAPTER 13: OBTAINING SOCIAL INVESTMENT

Raising investment yourself or through a social finance provider

If you want investment in your social enterprise, you have the option of either finding the investors yourself or going through a social finance provider (who either invests in your organisation themselves or finds individuals who will invest for you).

If you decide to raise investment yourself you can approach individuals who know your organisation, promote it more widely or use one of the crowdfunding sites. The only issue around raising investment yourself is trying to avoid the cost of having to do an FCA authorised share offer. If you want to avoid this then you need to fit within one of the exemptions, such as Common Interest Exemption (where the people investing are already known to your organisation), or by approaching individuals who are deemed to be Sophisticated Investors or High Net Worth Individuals.

There are a number of social finance providers that specifically want to invest in social enterprises. Most consider the social returns (social value) you achieve as well as the financial returns you can offer. If you are working with business angels you may find that they are solely interested in financial returns, whereas philanthropists may be more interested in the social returns. If you want to secure investment from one of the social finance providers it's important to start preparing your organisation for this 2-3 years before, and connect with the providers at least 12 months before.

Case study: Citizen Coaching CIC

Citizen Coaching is a great example of an organisation that has had a range of different investments and grants to help the organisation expand. Here, Martin Hogg, CEO at Citizen Coaching explains:

I set up Citizen Coaching because I was very unsatisfied in my corporate job, nothing seemed to matter but the numbers: people seemed to be increasingly an after-thought and in a growing command and control culture I felt that my skills weren't being put to best use. Around the same time I volunteered helping young people with multiple complex needs, using my coaching skills. I saw the power that coaching and counselling were having in my local community, and I was hooked!

There have been several challenges as the organisation has grown including adding extra employees, crossing the VAT threshold and moving to bigger premises but the biggest challenge was the access to quick affordable finance to scale up our proven model. The high street banks still don't understand the social enterprise model well enough and social lenders went through the phase of not wanting to lend below £250,000.

The culture of these large loans meant that lenders wanted complicated forecasts and detailed 5 year plans. Fortunately, Citizen Coaching CIC won through to Unltd's Big Venture Challenge supported by Big Lottery. Over the course of a year we worked with David Bartram from Unltd and Karen Leigh-Anderson from ClearlySo to identify funders and to develop both a robust business and financial plan in the language of lenders that enabled us to secure funding from our preferred lender from the offers we got, which was The Key Fund.

In running a social enterprise, the balance between trading and grants/funding is a source of great debate. In the early days we were very adamant that we would be primarily a trading social enterprise, often with 85-90% of income from trading in the early years. In hindsight we could have sought some grants and funding in the early days that may have got us to where we wanted to be quicker.

We are looking to scale up to work with 30,000 people a year. Within ten years we aim to be the recognised specialist in Anger Management working with 20,000 people a year through our social franchisees. We seek to be a leading provider of counselling in the West Midlands providing 100,000 quality counselling sessions a year.

The key piece of advice I would offer other social entrepreneurs is find support and a good peer network right from the start. Don't recruit another you – look for complimentary skills. Ask for help rather than figuring out it all yourself, and look to trade but also look for grants and funding.

Citizen Coaching is a Birmingham based social enterprise established in 2005. We enable adults and young people to live better lives by accessing timely, affordable and jargon-free counselling, anger management, personal development coaching and employment skills delivered by a friendly professional team.

At the frontline, Citizen Coaching trades as:

- Birmingham Counselling Services – a counselling and psychotherapy practice with a choice of ten trained practitioners who work with people experiencing difficulties and distress in their lives to bring about effective change or enhance their wellbeing.
- Citizen Click – a digital marketing service 'making digital media that little bit easier' for businesses and charities through social

media training, web design and video production.

- Anger UK – a package of 'train the practitioner' anger management workshops, weekly classes, online training, DVDs, CDs and books for counsellors looking to expand the range of services offered to clients.
- Citizen Home - an independent gift and homewares shop located in Birmingham's Jewellery Quarter.

www.citizencoaching.com

www.facebook.com/citizencoaching

@citizencoaching

@martinhogg

Make sure your social enterprise is investable

Key things investors look for are that the social enterprise has a track record of surpluses, has confirmed future income streams and revenues, has a solid business plan, the entrepreneur is receiving a wage (so that the surpluses are not a result of this person doing the work for nothing) and the social enterprise is not dependent on one individual for its success.

Pick the right type of investment

Nowadays there are a plethora of options available to social enterprises looking for investment. It is often all too easy to pick the wrong type of investment – and go with the first offer. My advice is to look at the pros and cons of each investor for your organisation.

The Charity Commission provide guidance for charities looking for social investment. In addition, The Charities (Protection and Social Investment) Bill was introduced in the House of Lords on 28 May 2015 which allows charities to make social investments themselves. This provides an opportunity for other charities and social enterprises as many charities have large cash reserves that could be invested instead.

Don't sell your soul – get the right investor and the right return

Make sure you get the right type of investor. Investors range from those that are completely hands off and just want a financial return, to those that are looking for more of a partnership with involvement in the business strategy and decision making. If you have established the social enterprise yourself and always made the strategic decisions letting go and having an investor involved in decision making can be difficult.

Also, the other part of selling your soul is making sure you get the right level of investment in comparison to the financial return they require. Think about whether you want to give away a chunk of the ordinary shares and lose ownership of the social enterprise, or give away a large proportion of the surpluses that could be used to deliver more social good servicing your loans or dividend payments. Getting the level of investment and financial return right are crucial for the future success of your social enterprise. By supporting your investor to understand about the social impact you deliver, you may be able to reduce the financial return they require, or alternatively specifically look for social investors who are interested in social impact already.

Connect early

Connect with investors before you ask for investment. This is my all time top tip for organisations looking for investment. All too often they contact an investor when they are ready for investment, rather than getting to know the investor over a period of 12-18 months. Think of it as dating one another to make sure they know about you and you know about them before you take the plunge and get married.

Consider the Tax Reliefs

If you obtain investment from an individual rather than through a business then there are a number of possible tax reliefs available to your investors providing they are paying tax.

Social Investment Tax Relief

For social enterprises that are set up as a charity, CBS or CIC, Social Investment Tax Relief (SITR) is available for both debt (loans) and equity (share) investments, and provides the individual with 30% of their investment as income tax relief, as well as providing relief against any capital gains. By offering investors a 30% sweetener your investment is more attractive and also the investor may forgo any return for the first one or two years on the basis that they have already received 30%.

Tax Relief on Share Investments

For organisations looking for investment through shares there is also the Seed Enterprise Investment Scheme (SEIS) and Enterprise Investment Scheme (EIS). SEIS is better than SITR as investors can obtain 50% tax relief providing it meets the criteria. If your investment does not meet the criteria for SITR or SEIS, then it may be eligible for EIS which offers investors 20% of their investment back as tax relief.

The tax reliefs also cover any increase (gain) in the shares value, so the gain is typically tax free providing the criteria are met. To access these reliefs for the investors your organisation must apply for approval from HMRC to confirm your investment opportunity meets the criteria.

Gift Aid

The most obvious tax relief is gift aid on donations to charities or Community Amateur Sports Clubs (CASCs) by individuals, which increases the income the charity or CASC receives. The charity or CASC can claim an additional 25% of the amount donated, up to a maximum of £2,000 in total, on small cash donations (up to £20 cash even where the individual donating did not complete a gift aid declaration). This means cash donations of £8,000 can be topped up to £10,000. Claims for gift aid are via HMRC, and the organisation must be registered as a charity or CASC with them. Where there is a completed gift aid declaration the organisation can claim gift aid on any value of donation.

The benefit to the individual arises if they are a higher rate or additional rate tax payer as they can reduce the amount of income they pay tax on at the higher/additional rate by the gross value of their donation. This means if a higher rate tax payer donated £100 and the charity received £125 with the gift aid added, the individual can claim a reduction in tax of £125 X 20% = £25. This means the donation costs the individual £75 but the charity benefits by £125.

Relief is also available on gifts of shares or securities, and gifts of land to charities. The tax relief includes exemption from capital gains tax and income tax relief based on the market value of the gift plus any costs of disposal.

For charities it is possible to claim SITR on the loan investment. When the loan is due to be repaid, the investor can decide to donate their investment to the charity rather than have it repaid. At this point the investor can also receive Gift Aid relief on the amount of the donation. On this basis, with an investment of £10,000, a 45% tax payer could receive £3,000 SITR, and then when converting the loan to a donation they could receive Gift Aid relief of £3,125. Clearly, from the charities' perspective donations are better, as they would receive £10,000 from the individual plus £2,500 of Gift Aid relief.

KEY POINTS

- Is social investment right for your organisation?
- Consider if the social investor is a fit for your organisation, and the balance of financial and social returns required.

- Identify if the investment will be eligible for any tax reliefs.

Further information:

For CICs interested in share offers: Raising Equity Finance for your CIC: A Guide to the UK Regulatory Framework and Exemptions, John Mulkerrin: CIC Association, July 2016.

For CBS and Co-ops interested in help with community share offers:
www.communityshares.org.uk and
www.communitysharesfund.coop

Social investors: www.bigissueinvest.com;
www.numbersforgood.com; www.sibgroup.org.uk;
www.thekeyfund.co.uk and www.clearlyso.com
(includes information on Clearly Social Angels)

Gift aid: www.gov.uk/donating-to-charity/gift-aid

SITR, SEIS and EIS: www.gov.uk/topic/business-tax/investment-schemes

158

CHAPTER 14: VAT

The Mysteries of VAT (Value Added Tax)

VAT is a complex area and I could write a whole book just on VAT. Suffice to say, in this book I have included some key aspects of VAT, along with some of the recurring questions I have been asked over the years. If you think any of these issues apply to your organisation I recommend you obtain professional advice to confirm the situation. My other key recommendation is that you do not ignore VAT – find out if it applies to what you are doing.

The background to VAT

VAT is not like other taxes – as you simply act as a collector of tax on behalf of HMRC with VAT. VAT is added to items when value is added to them – hence the name Value Added Tax.

You charge VAT on your VATable sales, and from this amount you are able to deduct the VAT you paid on items you have purchased. You then pay the net amount across to HMRC:

VAT on sales	£4,000
Less VAT on purchases	£2,500
VAT due to HMRC	£1,500

VAT Registration

You must register for VAT if your taxable turnover for VAT purposes is £83,000 or more. Please refer to the section on the different categories for VAT to identify if your taxable turnover is above this level.

You can voluntarily register for VAT below this level – and this is usually beneficial if you make a lot of purchases from suppliers who are VAT registered or the items you sell are zero rated.

If you are VAT registered and then decide you wish to deregister you can do this if your turnover is below £81,000. Once you are registered you are required to submit a VAT return each quarter and pay any VAT due.

Beware of artificially separating activities in order to avoid VAT registration. In the past businesses would set up a new company each time they got near to the VAT registration threshold, in order to avoid having to register for VAT. There are specific anti-avoidance rules to stop people doing this.

VAT Schemes

There are a number of VAT schemes available to organisations to help reduce the administration burden of being VAT registered. These include:

- Cash Accounting scheme – this allows you to account for VAT when you receive or pay the cash, rather than based on the invoice date of the sale/purchase. To be eligible for this your taxable turnover must be below £1.35 million.

- Flat rate scheme – this enables you to pay a fixed rate of VAT based on the industry sector you are in, rather than reclaiming VAT on any purchases you make. You can join this if your turnover is £150,000 or less.

- Annual accounting scheme – rather than submitting a VAT return every three months you submit just one return every 12 months. You still have to pay your VAT every quarter (or with monthly instalments) and then you pay the balance due once you submit the return. To be eligible for this you must have turnover below £1.35 million.

The different categories for VAT

The main difficulty for social enterprises is in deciding whether the income or sales they make are subject to VAT. This is important because it will help you to identify if your taxable turnover (income) is at the threshold for VAT registration, as there are penalties and fines for late registration.

VAT has its own way of categorising activities which is not the same as other taxes. For VAT you need to consider the following categories and identify which category each of your different types of income is in:

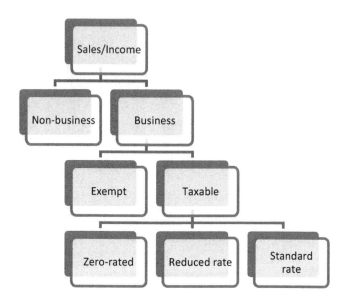

Non-business activities

Non-business activities are outside the scope of VAT – so no VAT is charged to the customers on these items but it also means you cannot recover any VAT on the purchases that are related to these activities. This is usually the case for activities that are funded by grants or donations – even if the funder provides you with a service level agreement or requires you to report on how you spent the grant and whether you achieved what you set out to do.

The main issue around grants arises when they are not genuinely grants and they are in fact contracts for services. This most frequently occurs when the public sector is providing a grant to a social enterprise and they have merged the wording from several different contracts or grant agreements they have previously used. The agreement may refer to grants, supplies, services etc as well as a service level agreement.

When faced with this mix of terminology, my recommendation is to actually read the agreement you have been given and before you sign it ask them to change any wording that makes the agreement ambiguous. You do not want to sign an agreement that you believe is a grant, only for HMRC to decide it was a contract. The reason being that, unless it is an exempt or zero rated supply you will be liable for the 20% VAT – and that will need to be paid out of the money you received – so you will have 20% less to spend on your activities. I also recommend if you are unsure you ask HMRC to review the agreement and confirm whether they consider it to be non-business or business for VAT purposes.

The other time supplies by social enterprises are seen as non-business is usually when they are provided at below cost or free as part of achieving a social or charitable purpose. This would include things like free meals for homeless people, support to people in poverty or pain. However, you need to be careful because if you provide something for free or low cost in order to attract customers it would not be seen as non-business, as it is for the benefit of your business activities.

Business activities

Business activities for VAT purposes are things you supply to your customers in exchange for some form of consideration – usually this is money but it could be an exchange where no money is exchanged – such as providing HR support in exchange for some catering. Business activities are split between exempt and taxable supplies.

Exempt supplies

Within business activities there are exempt supplies. A lot of social enterprises provide exempt supplies to their customers. Typical exempt supplies are:

- Education
- Finance
- Insurance
- Health
- Welfare
- Sports
- Art and cultural

If you are providing exempt activities no VAT is charged on the supplies and you can't recover any VAT on your purchases either – so it is similar to non-business activities. One of the issues I have come across is around vocational training. An individual I worked with was interested in providing vocational training and was planning to set this up in a CIC. In order to be able to treat the vocational training as exempt the CIC would need to be limited by guarantee because if it can distribute profits (like a CIC limited by share could do via dividends) it would not be eligible for this. It may be that you decide it is better to charge VAT on your training at the standard rate, rather than treat it as exempt, so you can recover VAT on your purchases. You would either set up a trading subsidiary to deliver the vocational training or use the profits from it for non-educational activities.

Under health and welfare services, things such as personal assistants, counselling, residential care, looking after vulnerable people, befriending, most nurseries and play groups, and after school clubs for children and young people. For cultural services this includes arts exhibitions and musical/theatre performances.

Taxable supplies

Taxable supplies are broken down in to three categories – zero, reduced and standard rate. Zero rated are where the VAT charged on the supplies is 0% - this is typically books and printed items, clothing and footwear for children, as well as the sale of donated clothing or footwear by a charity or its trading subsidiary, and certain items of food. The benefit of providing zero rated items is that you can recover the VAT on your purchases, even though you don't actually charge any VAT on your sales. This means you are always in a refund position, with HMRC reimbursing you the VAT you paid on your supplies.

If you are set up as a charity you benefit from being able to ask your suppliers to charge you 0% of certain items. This includes advertising (including the design of the advert) to the general public – so you could obtain this if you place a job advert, have a fundraising campaign or if you are advertising new activities. It includes any form of advertising such as in newspapers, online, TV, radio, on goods/items such as t-shirts, mugs, cards, bags etc.

Reduced rate supplies have VAT charged at 5% on them. Examples include mobility aids and installation of energy saving items such as solar panels in residential homes.

Standard rate supplies currently have 20% VAT on them, and include all items that don't have a specific exemption or other categorisation. The above lists of non-business, exempt, zero and reduced rated items do not include everything - just the most common items. If you are fundraising and obtain sponsorship depending on how much promotion the business receives, it is either treated like a donation (and non-business for VAT purposes) or the sale of advertising which is standard rated. To be treated as a donation the business would need to receive minimal promotion. HMRC typically looks at use of their logo, and the size and prominence of it.

Mixed VAT

Many organisations will have a mix of VAT on their different income sources, and will need to consider doing partial exemption calculations (if you have some exempt and taxable supplies), or a business/non-business split if you have both these types of supplies. In some cases, organisations need to do both a business/non-business and partial exemption calculation. If this applies please check you are doing it right, charging VAT on the right things, reclaiming VAT on the right purchases, and paying HMRC the right amount of VAT, as the penalties and fines for getting it wrong can be extensive.

A frequent area I have come across is organisations that set up or run a café. VAT is a very important consideration as the food and drinks you provide will have various VAT rates (zero, reduced and standard), and whether you serve them hot or cold, to eat in or take away also affects the VAT rate. Catering is usually standard rated because it involves a service as well.

The other thing to be aware of is that just because a type of income may not be subject to VAT doesn't mean it isn't subject to corporation tax.

KEY POINTS

- If you mainly sell to individuals then being VAT registered increases your prices as they can't reclaim the VAT, whereas if it is mainly businesses that are VAT registered themselves it will make no difference as they can recover the VAT.
- Consider if voluntarily registering is worthwhile if your main expenditure is staff salaries which do not have VAT on them – as you will have to charge your customers VAT but have very few purchases on which you can recover VAT.
- Check your sales regularly to make sure you register when you need to, as there are penalties for late registration once you reach the threshold.
- Make sure you categorise your different income correctly and get professional advice if you are unsure.

CHAPTER 15: SOCIAL VALUE

What is social value?

Social value became a popular phrase with the introduction of the Social Value Act in 2013. Prior to that social value was called social impact, impact measurement and impact reporting. These phrases are now used inter-changeably. In addition, Social Return on Investment (SROI), is a technique for measuring social value that is also frequently talked about.

But social value simply refers to the difference your organisation makes, the outcomes it delivers and the impact you have on the people you work with, society in general and the environment. In effect, what changes as a result of the work you do. Social value is about four key areas:

- Social impact – the changes you make to people
- Economic impact – the changes you make to the economy
- Environmental impact – the changes you make to the environment
- Community regeneration impact – the changes you make to the wider community

When you first set up your social enterprise you had a plan or vision for the difference you wanted to make, and reporting on your social value will let you know if you are actually achieving what you set out to do. If you aren't then it will tell you where you need to improve and make changes to your organisation.

Reporting your social value

I have always felt that it is important to tell the story of what you achieve as well as presenting a set of financial accounts. By having this balance between the finances and the outcomes and difference you have achieved, you can see the link between how you spent the money and what it delivered.

In order to do this, it is important to see the annual preparation of accounts as more than just a compliance exercise and legal necessity. Most social enterprises have accounts produced that fail to incorporate the story of what difference they have made. Charities tend to be an exception to this as they are required by Charity Commission to provide certain details of their activities and public benefit during the accounting period, and CICs have to produce a CIC Report, but neither of these require much detail of the impact the organisation has had.

Why bother reporting on your social value?

Reporting on your social value has the following benefits:

- A balanced and rounded view of what has been achieved - the financial story and the social story are presented jointly
- Powerful case studies and data on the outcomes achieved are available
- Access to information on potential savings to Government and SROI figures
- Greater clarity about what works and what doesn't work for the organisation, which supports business planning and identification of areas for improvement
- Staff are more involved and motivated as they can see the difference their work makes
- Greater brand awareness with customers and the local community
- Ability to effectively tender for public sector service contracts
- Provides funders with evidence of the difference you will make with their grant
- Demonstrates you are at the forefront of Social Value reporting

What is the Social Value Act?

The Social Value Act was introduced in 2013, and applies to all public services contracts over c.£113,000 (Central Government) and c.£173,000 (for other public sector bodies). Organisations and companies tendering for contracts have to consider the added social, economic, environmental and regeneration benefits that can be delivered through that public contract.

Most statutory agencies are being encouraged to implement the Social Value Act for all contracts regardless of value, so if you are measuring your social value already you will have evidence of how you can deliver more than the basic requirements of the contract.

Other changes

In addition to the Social Value Act, increasingly funders and commissioners are requesting SROI information and for specific outcomes to be reported on. The Big Society Capital Social Outcomes Matrixes are a useful tool for identifying outcomes and the possible information you would need to collect in order to evidence that an outcome has been achieved.

Simple ways to measure your social value

I am a great believer in not making social value measurement complicated. There are over 60 different approaches available for measuring your social impact and what this generally means is that people are confused, and frequently decide not to bother measuring their impact at all. This means they have no idea whether they are actually achieving what they claim to be.

If you want to find out if you are really as great as you think you are, then you need to ask your key stakeholders what difference you have made to their lives and what has changed for them. It doesn't have to be a series of questions, it could be getting people together in a room and asking them. Or alternatively you need to record this information on feedback or evaluation forms.

The best way to collect data is by starting to collect it straightaway, rather than trying to collect it retrospectively. One of the areas I find most beneficial is to look at asking questions around wellbeing if you are working with individuals. There are a number of free resources available, such as New Economics who identified a set of questions to use for changes in wellbeing.

Other outcomes that are relatively easy to measure are employment, training and volunteering outcomes, as you can identify where you have achieved these outcomes for individuals by getting them to complete follow up surveys. Typically, for every person you support in to employment it saves the public sector £9,800.

To start looking at your social value, think about the following areas, where you could collect information:

Economic:

- Do you employ local people?
- Do you pay the living wage to all employees?
- Do you provide employment for disadvantaged people and apprenticeships?
- Do you have volunteering programmes for employees to support community projects?
- How many individuals did you employ during the year?
- How many volunteers did you have during the year? How many hours of volunteering did they do?
- What training did staff undertake during the year?
- Do you have social enterprises or charities in your supply chain?
- Do you buy from local suppliers?
- How much did you spend locally?

Environmental:

- Do you recycle and minimise your impact on the environment?
- Do you purchase goods from sustainable or recycled sources?

- Do you know the amount of CO2 emissions your organisation generates?

Community regeneration:

- Do you support the development and improvement of community parks, places and facilities?
- Do you improve community cohesion?
- Do you work to reduce crime and disorder?
- Do you increase ownership and involvement of service users and the wider community?
- Do you increase the number of positive role models in the community?
- Do you help to set up other enterprises, or support individuals to become self-employed or employed?
- Do you increase community resilience by encouraging people to help one another more?
- Do you work closely with other social enterprises and charities?
- Do you donate to local charities or community groups?

Social:

- Do you help to improve family life?
- Do you improve living standards and reduce poverty?
- Do you work to reduce financial inequalities?

- Do you work to reduce health inequalities?
- Do you raise aspirations?
- Do you improve soft skills (communication, confidence, self-esteem, motivation etc)?
- How many people/organisations did you work with this year?
- What difference has your support made to their lives/organisations?

Using social value as a business improvement tool

Once you have measured your social value it doesn't end there. The whole point of social value is to identify the great outcomes you achieve and also to identify where things aren't working as well as you expected.

Once you know where the outcomes aren't that great, you can look at why that is, and then make changes to how you deliver or operate that element of your work, so you can improve the outcomes you achieve.

Measuring your social value should fit alongside your business planning processes, and provide vital information on your performance, a set of measures and KPIs you can track, and development areas.

Social Value Act – savings to the Government

One of the biggest benefits of measuring the social value you achieve is being able to identify potential savings to the Government. The way savings arise for the Government/public sector are through your intervention preventing something happening. Examples include:

- Costs of eviction avoided
- Reduced GPs appointments
- Less medication
- Less social services support required
- Reduced depression
- Reduced crime levels
- Reduced anti-social behaviour
- Reduced violence

The savings are always potential savings, as the reality is if money was saved in one area it would be spent on other types of support. The ideal situation is to have such an effective intervention that less money needs to be spent on curing/solving something, so more money can be put in to preventative work and services.

SROI (Social Return on Investment)

SROI is a technique for measuring your social value that converts the value in to a monetary figure. This is represented as £xx of social value for every £1 spent on your services/activities. The method involves finding financial values (proxies) for the outcomes you achieve. It is one of my favourite techniques for measuring social value because it converts it into a financial value that is easily understood.

At the moment SROI figures are not comparable between different projects and organisations, and the calculations are based on lots of assumptions which mean they can be manipulated. I am currently working on benchmarking an organisation's SROI so they can have an indication of how their outcomes compare to those of other organisations. This method involves committing time and resources to the data collection, analysis, identification of financial values and reporting.

Case study: Agewell CIC

Agewell is an example of an organisation that produces social impact reports and includes Social Return on Investment figures in order to evidence the value they provide to commissioners.

Deborah Harrold, CEO, explains why evidencing their social value was so important. Agewell is primarily funded by contracts with the local authority and health services. When those contracts come up for renewal we need to be able to show we have achieved what we said we would, and also that our services provide value for money particularly with all the budget cuts. This year we were able to evidence the potential savings to the local authority of our interventions, including our befriending service.

142 people received the befriending service, and to measure the difference it made to these individuals we captured data through SF12 and WEMWBS assessments. SF12 is a short form 12 question health survey that looks at quality of life, and WEMWBS is the Warwick-Edinburgh Mental Wellbeing Scale that is used to measure changes in mental wellbeing.

By collecting this data we were able to show that the people we supported were able to remain in their own homes for longer and there was a reduction in the number of falls, as well as improved social interaction, reduced isolation and improved mental wellbeing. All of these outcomes mean that people need to access reablement and health services less, there are less emergency admissions to hospitals, and there is no need to transfer to a care home.

By identifying financial values for these outcomes, such as the cost of treating an individual who has fallen which is £28,665 and the value of improving an individual's mental health which is £12,100, we were able to show the local authority how our programme was worth commissioning and funding. The SROI calculation showed a total social value of over £1.4 million. This meant for every £1 we spent we achieved £14.65 of added social value. With this report to back up and evidence the outcomes we were recommissioned to deliver the service again.

I would recommend organisations look at reporting on their social value and using SROI, as it can make such a difference when you are trying to secure contracts and grants.

Agewell is a social enterprise led by older people for the benefit of older people. Anyone aged 50 and over can become a member for free. As the population of the UK is an increasingly ageing population, the work Agewell delivers is more vital now than ever.

Agewell works with frail older people to support how they cope on a daily basis and how they interact with others, as well as improving their overall quality of life.

www.agewelluk.org.uk

@Agewellinfo

KEY POINTS

- Measuring the social value you achieve helps you to identify if you are achieving what you planned.
- Social value measurement is a business improvement tool that helps you to identify how you can improve your outcomes.
- Identifying the potential savings to the public sector assists you with evidencing value for money and the value of your interventions.
- Make it manageable and start by reporting on outcomes where the data is easy to capture.

Further information:

General Social Value information and examples of social impact and SROI reports:

http://www.goodfinance.org.uk/measuring-social-impact
http://inspiringimpact.org/measuringup/
https://socialvalueselfassessmenttool.org
www.socialvalueuk.org and
www.socialauditnetwork.org.uk

Big Society Capital Outcomes Matrix:
www.goodfinance.org.uk/impact-matrix

Measuring wellbeing and Financial Values:

www.neweconomics.org (Measuring Wellbeing Publication)
www.hact.org.uk/value-calculator
www.globalvalueexchange.org and
www.neweconomymanchester.com (Unit Cost Database)

CHAPTER 16: EXIT STRATEGIES

Begin with the end in mind

Someone once said to me "Begin with the end in mind.", and that advice has stuck with me as mentioned in Chapter 9. When you start your social enterprise and are writing the business plan, think about what will happen to your social enterprise when you are no longer involved.

This is important because most entrepreneurs are innovators and love the thrill of setting up a social enterprise. As the social enterprise grows the excitement can dwindle, as it becomes more about maintaining a larger organisation and less about innovating. You may also be ready for another challenge and to start something new.

You have the following options:

Find a manager

With this option you retain ownership (if applicable based on your legal structure) and you have someone to manage the social enterprise. This means you can potentially still receive an income from the social enterprise. If you are set up as a CIC Limited by Share then you could receive a dividend providing there are surpluses and you do not exceed the dividend cap. You could also continue to be involved by remaining on the Board of the organisation but ceasing to be involved in the day to day operations and management. This can be beneficial, but it can also keep the organisation trapped within its own past – as no-one dares to challenge your ideas and the future you see for the organisation.

Develop a successor

This is similar to the first option, except you have trained and developed the manager internally, and whilst stepping back from the organisation slightly you are still there to offer guidance. Eventually, you will hand over the social enterprise to this person. One of my personal beliefs is that you should train your staff to be better than you are, so they can do everything you can do and more. Because I took this approach I naturally developed a successor for my social enterprise.

Sell it or sell part of it

In this scenario you either sell the entire entity to someone else, or you sell part of it. This will not always be possible because of your legal structure. However, any organisation can sell part of its trading activities to another entity providing this is done at market value, and receive a goodwill payment in return. This is what I did with the accountancy part of my CIC. I sold that part, and I then decided to change the CIC's core services and objects – mainly because it was time to innovate and start over again, and because the services I provided had changed significantly from when I first started the CIC 9 years earlier. This changed the focus of the CIC to growing organisations, mentoring entrepreneurs and helping them to report on the difference they make in society through social impact reporting.

If you have a legal structure with shares you could sell your shareholding. In this situation you would receive a payment equal to the value of your share of the social enterprise. Many legal advisors have stated that because of the asset lock for CICs the shares can only be sold for their nominal value (which is the amount the shares were originally bought for and typically this is £1). However, this is incorrect, because it is not possible for a CIC to own the shares. The shares are owned by the shareholders, and this means the shares are outside the asset lock. The consequence of this is that shares can be bought and sold at any value, and the shareholder can make a profit on their shareholding.

For other legal structures, it is not always possible to sell the organisation. For example, with Limited by Guarantee companies it would not be possible to sell the company as there are no owners or shareholders. The company would simply transfer to new members – by the old members resigning.

Where you sell or transfer part of the organisation TUPE will apply to staff working in that part of the organisation. This is what typically happens when large public sector contracts are awarded to different organisations – the winning organisation acquires all the existing staff working on that contract, which can be costly if they are paid at higher rates than your current staff.

Merge

Merging your social enterprise is not a simple process. When I first started training as an accountant I worked in Mergers and Acquisitions, and there were so many variables and what seemed like tiny issues that could stop the merger happening. The most suitable mergers are where both organisations have had several meetings and staff have been involved in the process.

Crucial things to consider are:

- Do you have similar ways of working?
- Do you share similar values and ethos?
- How will it affect your customers/clients?
- How does it impact on your existing contracts and grants?
- What are the consequences for staff?
- How do you align staff salary rates, pensions etc.?
- Will you need to move to different premises/close premises?

- How do you merge your IT and reporting systems?
- Who stays on the combined Board and Management team?
- What are the costs of making these changes?

Close it

Whilst this may seem like an easy option closing a social enterprise is not simple, unless you are purely grant funded and close once your last grant has ended. Even then, there are still a number of important things to do.

To close down will involve notifying staff, volunteers, clients/customers and suppliers. You will need to sort out the legal and regulatory requirements of closing, which can take several months after the official close. There may potentially be client information that needs to be archived or stored for certain time periods after the closure, especially if you have had EU funding or contracts with public sector agencies. There will also be particular costs involved – such as covering pension liabilities, redundancy costs, final tax bills, possibly the cost of dilapidations/repairs on premises, and finding other support for your current beneficiaries/clients.

You also have to be careful if the organisation has an asset lock in place – which CICs and CBSs have, as well as all the Charity structures. This prevents them from transferring assets to other types of organisations at less than market value, and would mean any assets would need to be sold prior to the closure of the organisation. Any remaining funds in the bank account after taking in to account all the closure costs then need to go to another asset locked body.

KEY POINTS

- Plan in advance.
- Get the appropriate legal, HR, tax and financial advice.
- Start having conversations early.
- Don't make it public until agreement is reached to avoid alarming staff, customers or commissioners etc.
- Be aware that you may be required to help with the transition for several months before you can finally leave.

CHAPTER 17: THE FUTURE OF SOCIAL ENTERPRISE

The State of the Sector Now

Depending on the definition used for social enterprise there are between 70,000 and 741,000 social enterprises in the UK! Regardless of the exact number, one thing is for certain, social enterprise is a growth sector. More people are choosing to set up social enterprises each year.

BIS Social Enterprise Survey

The Department for Business, Innovation and Skills (BIS) used the following to identify if a small/medium enterprise (SME) was a social enterprise:

"The criteria applied for an SME to be classed as a social enterprise are:

• the enterprise must consider itself to be a social enterprise;

• it must not pay more than 50% of profit or surplus to owners or shareholders;

• it must not generate more than 50% of income from grants and donations (or, equivalently, it should generate at least 50% of income from trading); and

• it should consider itself either 'a very good fit' or 'a good fit' with the following statement: 'A business with primarily social/environmental objectives, whose surpluses are principally reinvested for that purpose in the business or community rather than mainly being paid to shareholders and owners'."

The findings from the survey by BIS in 2014 showed:

There are around 741,000 UK social enterprises in 2014, and this is 58,000 more than in 2012. 195,000 of these organisations employed at least one person, with a total of 2.27 million people being employed in 2014. The number of employees had increased by approximately 300,000 since 2012.

Social enterprises are more likely than SME employers overall to be in the food and accommodation, health, and arts and leisure sectors. Social enterprises are also more likely to be led by women and those from minority ethnic groups and are less likely to be entirely male led. Social enterprises are more likely to work in the most deprived 20% of areas, and less likely to work in the least deprived areas.

In 2014 75% of social enterprises were profitable, and reported increasing their turnover and number of employees in the previous year.

The biggest obstacle for social enterprises continues to be access to finance, particularly to finance expansion and growth. 49% of social enterprises had difficulty obtaining finance, and 31% were unable to get the finance they required.

Social enterprises are more likely than all SMEs to have individual consumers as their main type of customer (58% vs. 43%), and less likely than average to work mostly for private sector businesses (30% vs. 45%).

SEUK State of the Social Enterprise Sector

These figures from BIS are derived in a different way to the SEUK State of the Social Enterprise Sector 2015 data, which showed:

"The UK is viewed as a pioneer of social enterprise and the associated practices of social investment and social value. Government statistics identify around 70,000 social enterprises in the UK, contributing £24 billion to the economy and employing nearly a million people. Since 2005, over 11,000 Community Interest Companies have been founded, and the last five years have seen significant development of social investment to support the growth of this movement."

SEUK found that 49% of social enterprises have been around for five or more years, and 35% are less than three years old, and the rate of new social enterprise start-ups is more than triple that of SMEs.

76% of social enterprises were profitable or at breakeven, and 52% increased their turnover in the last 12 months. One of the most important things is that nearly three quarters of the social enterprises surveyed generate 75% of turnover from trading.

Social enterprises are also more likely to be women led than SMEs, have Black Asian Minority Ethnic Directors and have Directors with disabilities.

CIC Association's Survey

The CIC Association's 10 year survey of Community Interest Companies (CICs) in Spring 2016 found the following:

- 71% use volunteers
- Over 40% employ 2-5 people
- 55% have a local community of interest
- The average monetary value to replace social outcomes commercially is £310,000 per annum
- 60% increased turnover in the previous 12 months

- Over 75% provide services to the general public
- 30% funded the start-up costs from personal savings
- Over 30% had sought finance for working capital in the last year
- Over 40% of those trying to raise finance in the previous 12 months failed
- 25% state Grants as a principal form of income
- Nearly half of those surveyed get 80% or more of their income from trading

Whilst the data from these surveys shows slightly different figures, one thing is clear – social enterprise is a growth sector. More people are setting up social enterprises, more social enterprises are generating surpluses and more rely on trading rather than grants for the majority of their income.

The future of social enterprise

My belief is that in the next 10-15 years all businesses will be social enterprises – whether by officially amending their governing documents to incorporate a social purpose or by just being more socially conscious. There are more and more commercial businesses that deliver enormous social good, through their corporate social responsibility programmes, and this trend is unlikely to reverse as brands that have done this have seen growth in their sales. Consumers care that the company cares, and this is an increasingly important buying decision.

The issue is where does this leave a small social enterprise, who rather than competing with other social enterprises, is now having to compete with big multi-national companies that can shift strategy, develop products and services rapidly, and have £millions to spend on marketing and advertising? Should social enterprises try to compete?

My thoughts are that this is a positive thing for social enterprises, because it will force them to build a community and loyal customers, and to enhance their quality so they deliver the same or better quality than businesses. Interactions are increasingly about connection and people, and that is where social enterprises that operate locally have the power over anonymous multi-national companies.

The recent win by Virgin of a public sector contract from a CIC shows how feasible it is for businesses to evidence their social value and additionality well, whilst also having the resources and power behind them to offer more than a social enterprise can. I recently read an article, and it talked about a company that had a range of programmes for training people, offered employment to young people, ex-offenders and other disadvantaged groups, worked with numerous charities and had regular fundraising events, as well as having its own separate charity. The article said you would think this is a social enterprise wouldn't you? But it's actually McDonalds.

These examples show the power of large corporations to effect change globally. But it doesn't diminish the power of social enterprises because they are still making a difference. Through my own business I employed young people and trained them to be accountants, but the large multi-national accountancy firms employ hundreds of young people each year to train as accountants. It isn't the scale of what you do, it's about if you make a difference to someone's life. If you do that then competition becomes irrelevant. Social enterprises and multi-national companies might have very little in common in terms of how they operate or their values, but if 1,000 people's lives are changed then surely it's a good thing?

There was much debate when the CIC Regulator was considering increasing the dividend cap from 20% of the paid up share value to 35% of the distributable profits. The concern was that individual shareholders would take 35% of the CIC's profits out of the company each year, rather than using the profits to benefit the community the company was set up for. But the logical argument to this concern was as follows – by being a CIC rather than a standard limited by share company, 65% of profits are used to provide community benefit. If it wasn't a CIC there would be no community benefit at all, so isn't it better for up to 35% to go to individual shareholders so 65% can be used to do more social good?

Making it a legal requirement

Through the Corporate Social Responsibility (CSR) agenda it is likely that companies will be required to report more information on how they affect people, society and the environment in the future.

Whilst the UK has been at the forefront of social investment, we seem to be behind other countries when it comes to legislation for reporting on the difference companies make. Around the world a number of countries already require companies to report around Corporate Social Responsibility.

In France there are legal requirements for social reporting that have applied to large companies since 2001, and these were subsequently amended in 2012 to apply to all companies with over 500 employees. The reporting includes over 40 areas around social, environmental and sustainable development, based on a number of international CSR guidelines including the Global Compact, ISO26000, the Guiding Principles of Human Rights and Business, the OECD Guidelines for Multinational Corporations and the Global Reporting Initiative.

In South Africa from 2010 onwards companies listed on the Stock Exchange in Johannesburg are required to produce an integrated report that includes social, environmental and economic information as well as financial, and similarly, in Singapore, listed companies will have to do the same by 2016. India requires companies to allocate 2% of their profits to social and environmental projects if their profit is over $830,000.

The EU is going to make reporting mandatory for around 6,000 large companies in EU member states, but this still means the majority of companies would not be required to report anything. The reporting would include social, environmental, employee matters, diversity information and human rights matters. Denmark has already made this mandatory.

The Sustainable development goals

In September 2015 world leaders adopted the 2030 Agenda for Sustainable Development during the United Nations Sustainable Development Summit. This Agenda includes 17 Sustainable Development Goals with the aims of ending poverty, fighting inequality and injustice, and tackling climate change by 2030.

The 17 areas of the sustainable development goals are:

1. No Poverty
2. Zero hunger
3. Good health and well being
4. Quality education
5. Gender equality
6. Clean water and sanitation
7. Affordable and clean energy
8. Decent work and economic growth
9. Industry, innovation and infrastructure
10. Reduced inequalities
11. Sustainable cities and communities
12. Responsible consumption and production
13. Climate action
14. Life below water
15. Life on land
16. Peace, justice and strong institutions
17. Partnerships for the goals

To me these goals are aligned with social enterprise perfectly, and this is why I believe more businesses will become social enterprises, as they recognise their ability to impact positively on their communities and the environment.

Final Words

It is my hope that every social entrepreneur and social enterprise recognises the power they have to change the world, and that consumers continue to make positive and informed purchasing decisions. Once consumers refuse to buy from corporations that pollute the environment, have poor staff practices and shift their operations around the globe to save money and avoid taxes, there will be no businesses that are not social enterprises. I look forward to watching with interest the future of social enterprise globally.

As you learn and work more in the social enterprise sector, you will realise, it flows through your veins and has changed you as a person. **Social enterprise is not something you acquire. It is something you become.** (Based on the quote from Wayne Dyer: Abundance is not something you acquire. It is something you become.)

Further information:

Social Enterprise: Market Trends. Based upon the BIS Small Business Survey 2014, Cabinet Office, 11th March 2016.

www.socialenterprise.org.uk (State of the Social Enterprise Sector, SEUK, 2015).

www.cicassociation.org.uk (10 year survey of CICs, CIC Association, March 2016).

Sustainable development goals:
https://sustainabledevelopment.un.org/?menu=1300

If you can imagine it, you can achieve it. If you can dream it, you can become it. *William Arthur Ward*

GLOSSARY

Budget – an estimate of income and expenditure over a specific time period – usually a year.

Business plan – a document that sets out how an organisation will achieve its goals.

Cash-flow forecast –an estimate of the timings of expected inflows (receipts) and outflows (payments) of cash usually over a year, typically on a monthly or quarterly basis. It helps to identify if there will be shortages of cash and to plan for these.

Charity – an organisation with charitable purposes and with a public benefit.

Community Interest Company (CIC) – a community that is set up to benefit a specific community.

Community Benefit Society (CBS) – organisations that trade to benefit the community.

Company Limited by Guarantee – a company that has members rather than shareholders.

Company Limited by Share – a company that has shareholders who own and control it.

Consortia – two or more partners working together to access larger contracts and commissioning opportunities.

Co-operative – businesses that are owned by their members and trade for the mutual benefit of their members.

Crowdfunding – a way to raise finance for projects and initiatives from a large number of people, who either donate, lend or invest.

Debt finance – a form of finance where the organisation receives a loan that is repayable.

Dividends – the proportion of surpluses that are paid out to shareholders.

Enterprise Investment Scheme (EIS) – a tax relief scheme for individuals who invest in small companies that are not listed on a stock market.

Equity investment – investment by buying and holding shares in the organisation, usually with the expectation of receiving dividends.

Gift Aid – a tax relief for individuals to encourage donations to charities.

Grant – a sum of money given by a grantmaking body, funder or other organisation for a particular purpose.

Investment readiness – when an organisation can demonstrate it is ready to take on and utilise investment, and meet the requirements of the investor.

Loan – a sum of money that is borrowed and is expected to be paid back, usually with interest payable as well.

Quasi-equity – debt finance that has some characteristics of equity investment.

Social enterprise – a business with a social purpose, where surpluses are mainly reinvested for that purpose rather than paid out to owners.

Social entrepreneur – an individual who runs a business with primarily social goals.

Social impact – the impact or difference that your organisation has on people and the planet.

Social impact measurement – the process of measuring and evidencing the difference your organisation makes to people and the planet.

Social investment – investment that seeks social returns as well as financial returns.

Social Investment Tax Relief (SITR) – a tax relief for individuals who invest via debt or equity in eligible social enterprises.

Social Return on Investment (SROI) – a method of measuring your social impact that assigns financial values to the differences your organisation makes.

Social value – the social, economic and environmental value your organisation creates.

Value Added Tax (VAT) – a tax on products or services that is added to the sale's price at each stage where value is added.

INDEX

Printed in Great Britain
by Amazon

85698749R00129